"In his powerful debut, Trey Ferguson reminds us of the liberation that can be found when we value the art of speculation; when we allow God to be bigger than we can fully capture; and most of all, when we bring our true, full selves to the theological table. With honesty, wit, and creativity, *Theologizin' Bigger* is an invitation to revive our imaginations so that we may walk into the way of salvation—into the healing process of rehumanization."

Kat Armas, author of *Abuelita Faith* and host of *The Protagonistas*

"*Theologizin' Bigger* grants followers of Jesus the permission to re-engage their imaginations in the life of faith. It is a hopeful resource for those who find themselves amid questions, doubts, and shifts in their faith. Through deft observations, skillful storytelling, and his distinct voice, Trey Ferguson invites readers to bring their whole selves to their worship, get comfortable in wrestling with their current or past paradigms, and discover the courage to trust that God is good."

Kate Boyd, author of *An Untidy Faith: Journeying Back to the Joy of Following Jesus*, creator of the *Threaded* Bible studies, and host of *Untidy Faith*

"Prophets help people to see God—who God is, what God is up to in the world, and what God expects of us. Trey Ferguson is a prophet because he helps to dismantle the barriers manufactured by ecclesial gatekeepers. Yet, *Theologizin' Bigger* is not merely an indictment of status quo Christianity; it is a treatise on liberation. *Theologizin' Bigger* is a magnifying glass that does not make God bigger (that's impossible) but helps us to see God as bigger."

Dennis R. Edwards, PhD, Dean, North Park Theological Seminary

"Trey Ferguson's *Theologizin Bigger* is a timely invitation to transcend restricted theological imaginations and instead embrace the liberating heart of the good news. With prophetic fervor and pastoral wisdom, Trey dismantles oppressive hermeneutics while ultimately gesturing us toward our full humanity. Read this book!"

Drew G. I. Hart, Associate Professor of Theology at Messiah University and author of *Who Will Be A Witness?*

"What if the theologies we believed were constructed from the shadows of our lives? What if we looked at the dark nights of the soul and the topics we choose to ignore to find a better way to theologize? Trey's book is not a lamp to light our path but a guide to walk with us on the journey of reconstructing what we set our hope in. He combines his knowledge of history, doctrine, and culture with his life experiences to encourage us to build a spirituality that is more expansive, more inclusive, and seeks a more liberated world."

Camille Hernandez, trauma-informed specialist, author of *The Hero and the Whore*

"Trey Ferguson's *Theologizin' Bigger* is a remarkable contribution to the critical examination of theology and its practice. He captivates readers with his surgical communication style, effortlessly simplifying complex theological concepts and making them accessible in today's world. If you've been grappling with theology amid the challenges of our times, let Ferguson both encourage and guide you in what he aptly terms *Theologizin' Bigger*."

Dr. Terence Lester, Founder of Love Beyond Walls, author of *I See You*, *When We Stand* and *All God's Children*

"Prophets are rare in our culture and poets are needed in this challenging contemporary moment. Trey Ferguson is a poet and a prophet for such a time as this. Trey's book dares to mix theology and democratic yearnings with the ear of a gifted DJ. Each page puts down literary theological tracks that cause the reader to shout "Yes!" to the remixes curated on paper. Get on the spiritual democratic dance floor with DJ Ferguson and join the movement for a new future."

Otis Moss, III, Pastor, Trinity United Church of Christ, Chicago, and author of *Dancing in the Darkness*

"Trey has an uncanny ability to weave humor, theology, and storytelling together in ways that allow folks to feel at ease. *Theologizin' Bigger* is a beautiful testimony of the ways Trey understands God and seeks the wisdom that can be found in leaning into the nuanced places of others who don't necessarily believe what he does."

Robert Monson, co-director of enfleshed

"Every generation needs to discover new ways to relate to the Bible and faith in a modern world. It's exciting work when you have the right guides. Pastor Trey is one, and the imagination he brings in *Theologizin' Bigger* is what we need to chart pathways toward a wider liberation for all. Dig into this!"

Rev. Rohadi Nagassar, author of *When We Belong*

"*Theologizin' Bigger* is an incredible testament to a God worth believing in. Despite all the ways dominant Christianity has tarnished faith, Ferguson reminds us why the story of God has captured the imaginations of overlooked and exploited people throughout history."

Kevin Nye, advocate and author of *Grace Can Lead Us Home: A Christian Call to End Homelessness*

"It's a tall order, but I want four things in a book: brilliant writing, an education, laugh-out-loud humor, and inspiration to be a better human. In *Theologizin' Bigger*, Trey delivers on all four counts and then some. This book blew my mind, then my heart and soul. I'll read every word this man writes."

Marla Taviano, author of *unbelieve, jaded,* and *whole*

Theologizin' Bigger

Theologizin' Bigger

Homilies on Living Freely and Loving Wholly

Trey Ferguson

Foreword by Candice Marie Benbow

LAKE DRIVE

lakedrivebooks.com

Lake Drive Books
6757 Cascade Road SE, 162
Grand Rapids, MI 49546

info@lakedrivebooks.com
lakedrivebooks.com
@lakedrivebooks

Publishing books that help you heal, grow, and discover.

Hardcover ISBN: 978-1-957687-34-6
Paperback ISBN: 978-1-957687-36-0
eBook ISBN: 978-1-957687-35-3

Library of Congress Control Number: 2023947140

Cover design by Michael J. Williams
Illustration by Brandon Miltgen

In loving memory of
Ralph G. I. Ferguson, who taught me how to dream big.

To
Jasmyne, RJ, and Kylie, who keep my imagination active.

Now our knowledge is partial and incomplete, and even the gift of prophecy reveals only part of the whole picture! But when the time of perfection comes, these partial things will become useless.

—1 Corinthians 13:9–10 (New Living Translation)

If the concept of God has any validity or any use, it can only be to make us larger, freer, and more loving. If God cannot do this, then it is time we got rid of Him.

—James Baldwin

Contents

Foreword

Candice Marie Benbow

The B-I-B-L-E! Yes, that's the book for me! I stand alone on the word of God! The B-I-B-L-E! Bible!

AS A KID, I sang that song in full voice—not necessarily knowing what it meant. I just knew that I was a Christian and, as a Christian, the Bible should be the only roadmap for my life. If God is the sole source of my strength, then the scriptures would teach me how to access "Him" and all "He" has for me.

And, as a kid, that made sense. Though an inquisitive child, I didn't have a set of questions that caused me to side-eye the Bible (and the sermons preached from it). There were things that sounded strange, but at the same time I was singing that little diddy, my biggest concerns were circling everything I wanted in the Sears Christmas catalog and praying Santa would leave it all under the tree. Whether or not the Bible was the book for me would just have to wait until I was old enough to actually care.

There's a reason why the older saints of the Black Church would say, "just keep on living." It was their response to the ways younger folk would dismiss well-meaning advice as out of touch with the times. Essentially, they were telling us that if we were blessed enough to get a few more years under our belts, we'd see the value in exactly what they're saying. And many of us did.

The older we got, the more life happened. And the more life happened, the more unsustainable some of the biblical and theological lessons we were taught became. Racism, sexism, homophobia, transantagonism, classism, ableism, and so many other social ills set the world on fire and continue to flame. Add to that navigating personal challenges of family dynamics, mental health concerns, imposter syndrome, relationship drama, and fighting with everything you've got not to become your parents and sounding like them when stuck in traffic. Life for many of us ain't been no crystal stair. And when spiritual teachings and religious platitudes fall flat, the impetus is to walk away from it all.

Don't get me wrong (many have). Studies show that millennials and Gen Z are less likely to have affiliations with institutional churches and are more likely to embrace spiritualities that keep "religious foolishness" at bay. Today's deconstructionist movement aims to reclaim parts of our Christianity from the clutches of white supremacy and heteronormativity . . . which is a good thing. Yet, even as this needs to happen, I question just how invested many of the movement's leaders are in helping to actually *heal* the wounds religious trauma causes and chart new paths forward.

Enter Trey.

I'll be honest: as a Black feminist woman of faith, I've grown tired of hearing Black men talk about God. Partly because they were the only ones talking. Mainly because often what they said didn't make a lick of sense. And when I was engaged in my own personal campaign to hear fewer male voices, I encountered Trey's. I wanted to roll my eyes and ask, "Who *is* dude?" But I couldn't. In the words of those older Black Church saints, he was "talking right." Reading bell hooks, James Baldwin, and other Black writers, Trey was making the kinds of theological connections that help make faith live on the ground for everyday people.

And he is a pastor; he cares about folk in a way I hadn't seen in quite some time. Maybe since I was a child. There are many of us who can admit that, while the theology of our childhoods is eighty-five percent of the reason we're working through the traumas we have now, we also had pastors who really seemed to care about us back then in a way many seem too busy to care now. If we could find a way for this new generation of pastors to be more empathetic and intentional, grounded in theologies that don't kill our spirits and dreams, then we'd be cooking with hot grease! I see that synergy in Trey.

Plus, his social media clapback game is top tier and I love anybody who doesn't suffer fools on the apps.

When Trey told me that he was writing a book, I got excited. Admittedly, my primary concern will always be for the total liberation of my people. I thought about the many brothers who will be helped and *hoped* by Trey's theologizin'. There aren't many millennial Black men writing about God in the way Trey does. That matters, for a number of reasons. I'm not naïve enough to believe sexism is dead. I know there are many who will refuse to listen to women like me simply because we are women. And while I may believe they deserve a first-class ticket to the hottest parts of Sheol, thank God there are people who believe those guys are worth redeeming.

And attempt to redeem them, Trey does. In the book you're about to read, Trey offers something very important. He's taken this big and wide concept of our faith and broken it down into digestible stories that bring us back to why we fell in love with Jesus in the first place. And for those who were forced into that love during their childhoods, Trey offers opportunities to come to it on your own and discover it freely. He does not shy away from holding the institutions we've held dear accountable for the harm they have caused. And at the same time, he offers his work and words as a place where those same beloved institutions can begin to right their wrongs.

In this way, Trey is not only pushing us toward *bigger* theologies that can hold the totality of who we are. He is calling for us to embrace *better* theologies—theologies that fully honor our humanity and the God who fashioned us as good creations. And we are the better for it.

Whether you're still singing that biblical nursery rhyme in full voice without a care in the world, whether you haven't picked up a Bible and stepped in a church in years, or whether you find yourself somewhere in between, Trey wrote this book with all of us in mind. We were on his heart as he penned each word with purpose and precision. This tome is a labor of love. May we reciprocate that love by coming to each page with an open mind and receptive heart.

Candice Marie Benbow is a theologian, essayist, columnist, baker, and educator whose work gives voice to Black women's shared experiences of faith, healing, and wholeness. She is the author of Red Lip Theology: For Church Girls Who've Considered Tithing to the Beauty Supply Store When Sunday Morning Isn't Enough.

Introduction

I'M A THEOLOGIZER.

Some people would describe me as a theologian. I wouldn't argue with them on that particular front. But it's not a label I often apply to myself.

A theologian is something of a job description. People who specialize in theology or have dedicated a significant amount of time to the study of theology are often described as theologians. By most metrics, I'd fit the bill. I've just never been too interested in proving my bona fides on that point.

Simply put: I got a nerdy side, but not *on purpose*. I don't take pride in flaunting it. I'd rather you find out about that side of me the hard way than me tell you up front I'm a nerd and risk disappointing you by not being nerdy enough.

Theologizin' though? That's different. To theologize is to value the art of speculation. Theologizin' is theorizing about theological subjects. It's to wrestle with the attributes of God and God's relation to the universe and creation. It's the pursuit of a truth you're confident you'll never fully capture. When you theologize, you give religious significance to the stories you share and prioritize. I can't help it. I'm always doing that.

I first recognized I was a theologizer when I found myself turning random things into sermons in my head.

One time, I saw a spiderweb by my front door. Okay, let me fix that. I'd hate to start this book by telling half-truths. *My wife* found a spiderweb by my front door. She did *not* want that spiderweb to stay there. So she called me to do something about it. *That* is when I saw the spiderweb. I looked at the spiderweb and got lost in thought. I followed the thin, silky lines in the design. It was asymmetrical but still bore a beauty I struggle to describe. I thought about how this little arachnid was capable of building such a massive and intricate structure in such a short amount of time. It's not like I didn't use my front door several times a day. The more I thought, the more amazed I became over the fact that I simply lacked the capacity to build such a web. Sure, I only had two legs and a couple of arms (instead of the eight appendages the spider was blessed with), but I was *way* bigger than any spider I'd ever seen.

Yet here I was, going to work just to make money to pay bills and feed my family. And here was this spider, setting up shop in front of a house it ain't pay no bills in. Little critters would get trapped in this web. The spider would be able to eat because of the work it did with no training or student loan debt. *Just by doing what it was uniquely created to do,* that spider would be able to live a whole life.

That spider was preachin' to me.

I told my wife what I'd learned from that spider just like I told y'all. She looked at me with a blank stare and asked if I took down the web or not. That's when I realized I was probably doing too much.

I wasn't doing it on purpose though. I'm not even sure when it started, but the most mundane things turn into investigations. I'm always looking at the world around me and wrestling with what I learn about God and creation through these observations. I notice things and ponder past the point that most people would consider productive. I'm ascribing religious significance to all sorts of things in real time. I'm consistently filtering my religiously held beliefs through the lens of the things I experience on a day-to-day basis.

Theologizin' is a little more active than the image that the word "theology" stirs up in the imagination. You can study theology and become an expert. But theologizin'? That's an *action*. You can't theologize without breaking a sweat.

Studying theology is usually deliberate. You can go to a school of theology and get a master of theological studies degree. I've been to a couple such schools. This ain't shade against theologians. Remember, I'm a theologian too, depending on who you ask. Still, the label "theologian" can seem a bit exclusive at times. And if you own the fullness of your identity in the pursuit of theology? If you just "be yourself" as a theologian? You're liable to get a couple labels tossed your way. If you're doing theology as a woman? Now you're a *feminist* theologian. You openly Black? You're a *Black liberation* theologian. Are you a proud Black woman? You're a *womanist* theologian now. Apparently the only "normal" theology is the kind all the white dudes in the sixteenth century did, and everything else is a derivative.

I think everybody does a lil' theologizin' though.

The enslaved African people who heard one gospel of submission preached to them by their enslavers but understood that the God of the Exodus was the kind of liberator who heard their plight? They were theologizers.

The European pilgrims who took that same story of the Exodus and understood that God was with them as they left the only land they'd called home and sought prosperity in the "New World"? They were theologizin' too.

If you believe there is an active, divine force impacting the world around you, congratulations. You been theologizin' this whole time.

Theologizin' ain't just for the theologians. It's for everybody who's still thinking thoughts about God. Good thoughts. Bad thoughts. Skeptical thoughts. Undoubting thoughts. Old thoughts. New thoughts.

When you're willing to sit with those thoughts and follow where they lead you, I'd call you a theologizer.

I think a lot of overtly religious and religious-adjacent people have been theologizin' since forever. It's how we end up organizing around things like religion. Theologizers have been at the forefront of religious schisms too. And people who up and leave faith systems behind? In my experience, they usually only do that after quite a bit of strenuous theologizin'.

Theologizin' in certain spaces can cost you a whole lot.

———

A LOT HAS BEEN made of the shifting religious landscape in recent years. The Europe that we see right now is less overtly religious than it was a few centuries ago. At the time of this writing, religious identification in the United States has been in decline for the last five decades. The fastest growing religious identification in the US is the "nones"— people who self-identify as atheist, agnostic, or nothing in particular.

I've got a few theories as to exactly why that is. As life (particularly in the West) has become more global, we have more access to diverging viewpoints than we've ever had. Some of the viewpoints and experiences we encounter are *extremely* difficult to reconcile with the beliefs that have been placed on the table before us. Faith communities with rigid boundaries and orthodoxies might feel unaccommodating to people who are trying to sort through their beliefs in a world that is constantly challenging their own lived experiences. Just as the printing press changed the world (both sacred and secular) in the sixteenth century, current mass-media developments are impacting the speed at which we receive and process information in ways that might've made the patriarchs dizzy.

Also, some of the theology of the church seems irrelevant to contemporary society. Theology speaks to contexts. The work of a good theologizer is to take an inherited theology, wrestle with how it speaks to *the current context*, and present it in a way that honors tradition while acknowledging the current day. And some communities just don't like that kind of work.

Some people feel forced to make a choice. Either they pretend that inevitable change is not happening around them for the sake of belonging to a community of faith, or they leave so they can lean into that change without the shame that comes from that very community when reconsidering and adjusting beliefs. Many of those people are choosing the latter.

I do think there's a difference between the things that people *believe* and the communities they say they find *belonging* in though.

And that's why this book exists.

I think there are plenty of people in religious communities who don't fully know what they believe. They know what to *say* they believe. But, for the most part, they don't live in absolute silos and are getting a lot of the same information and have a lot of the same questions.

Likewise, I think there are a lot of people who have left religious communities behind even as they hold a curiosity (and maybe even a hope!) for the Divine.

While I am not shy about the fact that I am a Christian minister, this book is *not* intended to be an explicit invitation to conversion or discipleship. I'm happy to walk you through what that might look like or mean for you, but that's not what this particular book is about. This book is an invitation to theologizin' a little differently than we may have felt was permissible.

When I speak of diverging viewpoints, faith communities with rigid boundaries, irrelevant theologies, and contemporary contexts, I'm trying to name a convergence of factors that present obstacles for theologizers. It's easy to look at these factors and think that we have to give up theologizin' altogether, or that we have to ignore large parts of ourselves in order to keep being theologizers.

This book is about a third option. You don't have to ignore your nagging doubts and honest questions. You don't have to check any part of yourself at the door. You don't have to stop theorizing or theologizin'. You can theologize *bigger*.

Some Housekeeping Notes

BEFORE I KNEW I was a writer, I knew I had stuff to say. And before the podcasts and newsletters, I said a lot of that stuff on social media. I was microblogging before I knew that's what it was called.

You'll notice that every one of the chapters in this book begins with a quote. Those quotes are actual social media posts I've made over the years.

Before I knew myself as a theologizer, I'd been theologizin' on the platform formerly known as Twitter. I know it's been rebranded, but whether it's Twitter or X or whatever else, I did most of my theologizin' on "Twitter," so that's what I'll be calling it here. I open these chapters with those posts because the first rule of theologizin' bigger (and right now, it's the only rule . . . I'm still making these rules up) is to bring your whole self to the table. If it weren't for these tweets, I'd have never known I was a writer. Truth be told, trying to squeeze thoughts into 280 characters or less took a fair amount of creative energy. I was theologizin' in spurts without knowing what to call it. So I'm starting where it all began even as I move into the new things and spaces I've been called to.

In addition to the tweets at the beginning of each chapter, you'll notice the book is split up into four sections.

In the first section (B.I.B.L.E.), I spend some time talking about how the Bible interacts with our faith. A lot of Christians see the B.I.B.L.E. acronym and default to "basic instructions before leaving earth." It's important to note that I'm not trying to condemn the Bible in anything I write here. I read the Bible every single day—and not to tear it apart. I actually *enjoy* reading the Bible. It makes me feel more connected to people in the ancient past, the recent past, and the present. I feel more connected to God and creation as I read the Bible. But no longer through the "basic instructions before leaving earth" lens. Instead, I now recognize the Bible as "books inspired by life's experiences."

The second section (The White Man's Religion) speaks directly to the tension that I've experienced in my life as a Black man in the United States and as a Christian in the West. These are both parts of my identity that I inherited before affirming them. I was born and named as Black before I had any say in the matter. I was born into a Christian family before I decided to be one. Holding my faith with any sort of integrity has required a commitment to learning and unlearning the ways that race and the Christian faith have shaped each other over the past few centuries. From that process of learning and unlearning, I share a few thoughts about what theologizin' bigger might look like in light of the way that white supremacy has defined so much of what we accept as Christian thought in today's world.

The third section (A State of Confusion) deals with the dissonant ways we often talk about Christianity in our contemporary context. Scripture plays a significant role in shaping our understanding of faith, but so do things like reason and experience. When our reason and experiences lead us in a different direction than the faith we're fed, it leads to a lot of confusion. It can even lead to an exodus.

In the final section (Faith That Shapes Tomorrow), we look at what theologizin' bigger might mean for the future. Generations down the line, people will look at the theologizin' we're doing *right now* to try to make sense of the ways they think about God. We can lay a foundation that leaves them as isolated, close-minded, and confused as ever. Or we can try and lay a path that leads them to wholeness.

My prayer is that we'd help lead everyone to wholeness.

Part I

B.I.B.L.E.
(Books Inspired by Life's Experiences)

1

The Very Word of God

If God didn't author every word of the Bible with their very own hands, then we have to introduce shaky things like reason and perspective when we read.

PEOPLE TRIED TO TELL me about seminary. I even heard pastors jokingly refer to it as "cemetery." Looking back, I'm not sure if they were actually joking, or if it was one of those "laugh to keep from crying" situations. But I'd been warned: seminary wouldn't be gentle on my faith. Those warnings did not land. Because I'm hardheaded. I remember the day I found out the hard way.

"God does not have an autograph."

"There are no recordings of God."

I ain't know if my biblical studies professor was saved after I heard him say that. It didn't matter though. I couldn't spot a lie in what he said. I'd never seen God's handwriting. The urban philosopher Pusha T once autographed a bootleg CD for me on a flight we'd both boarded to Miami. I've seen his handwriting. I have never seen God's handwriting.

I've heard so many voices over the course of my life. I cannot prove beyond a reasonable doubt that any of them belonged to God. I do not think there is a forensics lab on the planet that can rightly identify the voice of God. And yet, so much of my faith depended on understanding each and every word of the Bible as the very words of God. What was I supposed to do with this faith now that I couldn't be certain about any of that anymore?

I should've listened. Seminary was the worst.

———————

I AM A PRODUCT of the Black Church. And while I'd never used the word "evangelical" to describe my faith, it is often a fair descriptor of some of the things that I was raised to value. One of those things is the centrality of the Bible. We take the Bible seriously. Though the Bible does not make this claim about itself, a central tenet of our belief is that the Bible is "the word of God." The Bible *does* say that all scripture is inspired by God, but the person who wrote those words didn't have the same Bible we do. The collection of writings we now call "the Bible" was loosely and unofficially defined for the first few centuries after the ink on the last of its pages dried. The Bible wasn't written as one single book. It is a collection of writings from multiple people, writing to diverse audiences in considerably different contexts.

But it didn't matter. Where I'm from? Interrogating the Bible was questioning God's word, and that's something you just don't do.

I wasn't too good at following instructions though. If there was room to ask questions, I was going to ask questions. And if there wasn't room to ask questions? I'd squeeze them where they didn't fit. I needed things to make some kinda sense. I found comfort in clarity. But getting there always got me accused of "questioning God's word." Jacob got a whole blessing and a brand-new name for outright tryna whoop God's tail in a mixed martial arts match one time (I know that story well—I spent a lot of time in God's word), but somehow I was out of pocket for having some questions every now and then.

I did not feel welcome where I could not bring my questions.

My questions are a part of me. I think I got it from my father, who never met a convention or expectation he wasn't willing to question. He was known for carrying a notebook full of graphing paper around, where he'd try to figure some things out and architect new things where the current things didn't make sense to him. We are two people largely defined by curiosity and wonder. Regardless of how uncomfortable or annoying other people found them to be, all the lessons I've learned in life are tied to questions. They show me where my insecurities exist. They guide me through curiosity and into growth. Leaving my questions behind would render me feeling stuck and incomplete.

Eventually, I took me and my questions out into the world. For some reason, people outside the church weren't as worried about me having questions. In fact, questions were encouraged. I discovered that many of them had the same questions. I'd found decent company among the questioners, and this was a balm to my curious soul.

But my people will always be my people. I still had people in the church. I still had people who walked with the word of God. The word did the talking while they journeyed alongside it, giving silent assent at times and enthusiastic affirmation in others, but still never questioning it. I traversed these two worlds clumsily, blurring the lines between the company of questioners of the word and guardians of the word. There were times I'd forget to check my questions at the door in the company of the guardians. Other times, I would forget to ask enough questions when I was with the questioners.

Things went on this way until I decided to just be *me*. Being me was at once the easiest and the hardest decision I'd ever make.

Deciding to be me was easy because being me was what I'd always felt led to do. This latent, unfulfilled desire was the source of most of my tensions. It was the force that dragged me against some grains. Being me meant listening to the voice calling me beyond the paths others had decided for me. In many senses, it wasn't hard at all to stop resisting that voice.

But deciding to be me also felt like a betrayal of my community. I felt as though being me would disappoint some people I deeply cared about.

Taking up the space that being my authentic self required seemed like it might leave me all on my own. That was an intimidating prospect.

The me that I decided to be was no longer concerned with how people felt about the case full of questions I carried around with me. The me that I decided to be was fine with the Bible meaning more to me than it did to so many of the questioners. Even as I felt like I was sticking out in whichever company I happened to find myself, I found freedom in being me. I'm glad I made that decision.

———

I HAVE A CONFESSION to make. The story about my professor telling me about all the admissible evidence—the actual recordings—God was careful enough to avoid leaving behind? That was from my second trip to seminary.

I remember when I made it to seminary the first time. It felt like it'd been a long time coming. But I made it. I was so excited to bring my questions to an actual university setting full of people who took the Bible seriously. Not just "word of God" serious, but also "what do we actually have here in this Bible?" serious. I was determined to be a serious thinker when it came to the Bible, because I'd proven to be a pretty serious thinker in everything else I cared about. My first professor tried to put a dent in that plan.

"What do you all make of the creation account in Genesis 1–2? Should we read that literally? Allegorically? Something else entirely?"

I was so excited. These are the types of questions I'd enrolled in seminary to wrestle with. And so I dove into the discussion with the vigor of a kid on Christmas morning.

My response: There are parts of the Genesis account that seem almost poetic. It's a wonderful account of the care God took in creating the earth and everything in it. At the same time, some things give me pause. If the sun wasn't visible until the fourth day of creation, then how were day and evening measured the first three days? Perhaps literal, twenty-four-hour days are not the main idea here. Is it any less impressive if God created the world over six million years instead of just six days? How much time would it take you to create something comparable?

I felt freer than I'd felt in a while as I shared these thoughts. I felt free because I was among all of my people. We were treating the Bible as the word of God, and we were having discussions about it. I got to bring my questions into a classroom with the guardians of the word! Freedom had finally led me to a place where I was comfortable. I felt like I fit here.

And I felt that way until my professor responded to these questions of mine. He accused me of hedging. Of lacking conviction. It was deflating. I replied to the question because I thought I'd found a space where I could grow. Instead, I found a space where part of me would need to suffocate another part of me if I had any hope of surviving. I recognized that I'd invested time and money in receiving an education that would not make room for my questions. I could've stuck to church for that.

MAYBE YOU ARE LIKE me. Perhaps you've long carried questions with you. Questions that you felt like you had to keep close to the vest. If anyone found out these questions traveled with you, they might think you were weak in faith. And when you are weak in faith, you become the prayer request instead of the conversation partner. You become the object of every apologist's wildest fantasy. You are robbed of the intimacy that binds community. In trying to more fully understand the faith that is supposed to make you more whole, you are made to feel as though you are more broken. Not the "only God can fix this" kind of broken, but the "your thinking is wrong, and mine is right" kind of broken. You begin to wonder if any of this is even worth it.

Beloved, it does not have to be this way.

There is a reason the Bible is shared in words that humans can send and receive. We are often bound by what we can perceive. To say the Bible is the word of God does not require us to reduce God to a human-oid creature that only communicates as we would expect a human to communicate. To be clear: imagining God as human certainly has its advantages. A human-God construct does not require us to activate our imaginations. Presenting God as something concrete—something per-ceptible enough to be captured in words—does us the favor of capturing the essence of the eternal, much in the same way that a vivid character description might do in a young adult fantasy novel.

But the eternal cannot be captured. Getting God to sit still long enough to capture a high-definition photo is an impossible task. You'd have an easier time sealing a cyclone in a jelly jar. The mere idea of God necessitates the reality of something grand existing beyond our plane of comprehension. We can only conceptualize the great beyond in glimpses and flashes. We can only describe the indescribable in metaphor. The word of God is a reality that cannot be contained in a book. But we can capture blurry parts of it. If blurry fragments are all that we have, cer-tainty becomes elusive.

Where certainty becomes currency, questions become contraband.

Two seminaries and some years later, I realize why questions are not always welcome in some spaces. Questions highlight the gaps in our understanding. They force us to lean into a reality in which unknown things must be confronted. Entertaining unknown entities in a quest to better know the Creator seems like hustling backwards. We've invested too much in constructing theologies and cultivating knowledge about God to spend so much time dabbling in the things we don't know.

But what if these constructs of knowing God are capable of prevent-ing us from experiencing God? What if these things that we don't know are invitations of the Almighty to catch glimpses beyond the blurry fragments and snapshots that we have compiled in this library we now recognize as the Bible? What if this limited, finite collection of writings is not even supposed to contain the fullness of the word of God? What might that demand of the thoughts we think about the Divine?

I'm not vain enough to presume I'm thinking new thoughts here. I suspect that ambiguity has always been a part of God-talk. That might be why a reader paying close enough attention can't get past the second chapter of the Bible before raising a question about whether animals were created before, after, or in the middle of the creation of the first humans. Perhaps leaning on the minutiae we believe we have grasped about God is not the path to our truest selves. Maybe dwelling in the details distracts us.

I FIND IT CURIOUS that the Bible allowed so many authors in a collection so important to setting the trajectory of a people. In my Protestant tradition, we acknowledge sixty-six books of the Bible. Within those sixty-six writings, who would dare to venture counting the number of fingerprints on those pages? In the collection known as the Psalms alone, a whole gang of psalmists are identified as contributors. That's to say nothing of letters like Hebrews, where no author is identified. And let's not get started on books where biblical scholars aren't so convinced that the author named in the book actually owned the hand moving the quill.

I won't lie to you: I feel like God chose an awfully sloppy process if the goal was for us to receive each and every single word as though it were spoken by the mouth of the same God. God could've given it all to Moses on Sinai that first time and provided a little more uniformity to all of this. But that is not what happened. Instead, we are left with a collection of various writings: wisdom literature, poems, songs, letters, teachings, sermons—and even some stories that seem a lot like what we'd now consider folktales. We even have some writings put in there twice. Either God is a sloppy editor, or the voice of the people was preserved in the text on purpose.

If God is a sloppy editor, then the Bible is of marginal value. If the voice of the people is preserved in this text, then the Bible is an invitation to seek God in our history, present, and future. And that is messy business. Where we detect God's activity in the past is deeply dependent on where we perceive ourselves to be in the present. Where we request God's intervention in the present is a commentary on the injustices we are willing to name. The future we hope that God is shaping is the antidote to the brokenness we sense right now. This makes theology a subjective task. In a contemporary religious culture where certainty and absolutes have often become the valued currencies, it's difficult to build around subjectivity.

Across millennia, linguistic shifts, religious reformations, political upheavals, and cultural revolutions, people have sought to write about God. Their reflections shed light on their specific circumstances. Their cultures are reflected in the language in which they choose to write and the terminology they employ. The symbols and stories they value in worship are communicated through various emphases, and how God directs their attention varies. The Bible is not simple. It is an invitation into the complex reality of human history, the story of a people, and the ways they have encountered and intuited the Divine intervening (or sometimes choosing not to intervene) in their circumstances. The Bible models how we ought to think about a God who set history in motion and lets us work out our own testimony.

I GET WHY SEMINARY was tough for me. My first seminary did not work out because I thought I was ready to theologize bigger, but theologizin' bigger isn't always seen as a faithful posture. My second seminary challenged me because I thought I was ready to theologize bigger, and I realized that my concept of bigger was not big enough. My first trip was rough because I was being taught by guardians who thought that questioners were dangerous. My second trip was rough because I was being taught by questioners who thought that guarding the word was dangerous.

The truth is that we have always had both. The questioners and the guardians provide necessary balance in the theological ecosystem. I look back on my academic journey as preparation for the world to which I was called to minister. I am committed to serving the church in a way that encourages the guardians to explore the wide world of questions. I am committed to showing up in the world in a way that encourages the questioners to entertain the possibility that some of what they seek might be found among the guardians. I am committed to accepting the invitation that the Bible extends. I am committed to seeking and pursuing where God is drawing us in our age and context.

Theologizin' bigger beckons us beyond binaries. It calls us to recognize two poles, plot the spectrum, and then exist outside of it. It disabuses us of the notion that the middle ground is holy ground and leads us to a land where the ground is altogether different and foreign. It demands that we think and communicate in new paradigms.

It is no coincidence that, as the disciples of Jesus awaited the next movement after his resurrection and ascension, the Spirit of God harkened back to Moses's first encounter with God. As Moses settles into life on the run in the wilderness, he notices a bush that is aflame but not consumed. As Jesus's followers accept the reality that their teacher has gone away, what looks like tongues of fire appear on each of them. Just as God called out to Moses through the bush of fire and directed him to speak of freer possibilities to a people in bondage, God empowers the incombustible disciples to speak to people of various nations about the freedom that exists beyond their current state.

But the miracle of God is not that the people of the nations would all understand the same language. It is not that their differences of language, perspective, and understanding were erased in order that one objective presentation might become the standard by which all others fall short. The miracle of the Holy Spirit enabled those who had walked with Jesus to speak in languages they had not known before. The Spirit of God did not direct the world to conform to the language of the disciples. The Spirit of God directs the disciples to bring forth the truth of God in ways that can be readily grasped by those in need of it.

The word of God is not relegated to the words we read from pages. The word of God is made manifest when God's beloved lean on God's Spirit in ways that lead them beyond their comprehension. The word of God is made manifest when I can communicate—to those whose native tongues are different—that God's desire is also for their wholeness. The word of God is made manifest when our differences are not barriers to God, but invitations for the Spirit of God to move in new ways. The word shows up where people can detect the Divine reordering things as we know them.

The word is made known in the person. It cannot be contained to the pages of scripture alone. It is embodied and incarnated. If the word is constricted to the pages, the gospel is neutered. As a Christian, I believe that God is made known in the person of Jesus of Nazareth. The Jewish teacher who took the actual words of scripture and said, "You have heard it said, but I say to you . . ." suggests that there is more to God than simply *knowing* the scriptures. The fullness of God is discerned in the reality of existence. The word of God is *experienced*.

The word is made known when the guardian and the questioner are cleaved back into one. It is not a matter of choosing to be either an inquisitive person or one who reveres the sacredness of a text or tradition. God's word is revealed when we allow our interrogation to illuminate our reverence and when our investigation is shaped by the stories we've lived. It is made known when we the questioners and guardians are not segregated into silos, but rejoined in communion.

The Bible collects the newspaper clippings of peoples in ancient times recording the instances where they have either seen the word made manifest or called on the word to set things right. The Bible invites us to make note of where the word appears in our midst and to bring it to bear where we cannot detect its impact. And we can only do that when we allow our experiences, reason, and perspectives to resume their rightful place in conversation with God.

2

The Bible Ain't No Car Manual

The Bible is not a car manual. You not gon' be able to search in the back for just any topic and find the chapter and verse to answer every question under the sun. Doing theology requires critical thinking skills.

THERE ARE TWO STATEMENTS that make me distrustful of a speaker: "trust me" and "the Bible is clear."

Let's be clear on one thing: the Bible is not simple. It is not a Magic 8 Ball. We don't get to ask it a question, shake it real hard, and find the answer. There is no standardized index of topics to search for each and every dilemma of our lives and find the corresponding book, chapter, and verse. The Bible will not tell us who to take to senior prom. It doesn't tell us how to vote in primary elections. There is no biblical rubric for settling the Jordan vs. LeBron debate.

The Bible will not absolve us of the need to put on our thinking caps. We are going to have to do some work.

It would have been pretty helpful if the Bible *was* a car manual. That could have prevented a few major schisms in church history. We could've avoided a few protests and reformations. We might have something resembling a single Christianity—as opposed to a plethora of divergent Christianities—if the Bible were a bit more straightforward. But it is not. So we have not avoided those schisms, protests, and reformations.

We do not have a monolithic Christianity. This is only a problem if uniformity is a virtue. Beloved, we have been given different minds for a reason. Between the world of biblical studies and the world of theology, there is the widest of gulfs. I love the Bible. I have been transformed by it. To this very day, I maintain a daily habit of poring over the literature of the Bible. My regimen typically involves a reading from the Hebrew scriptures—something from the Torah (instruction) or *Nevi'im* (prophets)—then something from the New Testament, then a couple of Psalms and a chapter of Proverbs. I'm not sure how many times I've read the Bible all the way through at this point, but it's certainly more than a couple of times. (My record is forty-six days from the beginning of Genesis to the end of Revelation—I just figured I should mention.) But my calling isn't necessarily that of a biblical scholar. I do not teach about the composition of the Bible and the many ways we approach it in an academic setting.

To be sure, I've been a student of many Bible scholars. Indeed, much of the way I engage with the Bible today is directly attributable to the work of brilliant scholars of the past and present. Drs. Jerome Ross, Wil Gafney, Mitzi J. Smith, Pete Enns, and Robert Alter are some of the many scholars who have impacted the way I engage with the Bible. I don't have any apprehensions about sitting with biblical scholarship. It just ain't my job. I'm a minister. Scholars work in isolation. It's a research-oriented job, where people build on the work of their scholarly peers and that of scholars before them to develop new levels of understanding with regard to complex topics. Scholarship is cool, but—ultimately—that's not what people need (or even expect) from ministers. It's a bonus that many of us offer. I'd go as far as to say that the best ministers value and incorporate the work of biblical scholars. My job is to take this super duper old book, see how the people who authored it have seen God revealed in their lives, and answer one simple question for the people I have the privilege of serving: *who cares?*

My task is to theologize. I consider a whole bunch of things (including—but not limited to—the Bible) and articulate how God shows up for us in a given situation. I look at our lives and try to piece together how God would direct us.

The Bible was written by many ancient theologians. But one thing they conveniently left out was a step-by-step guide on how the people who live on the other side of the planet—some two thousand to three thousand years after them—ought to live their lives.

———————————

CHRISTIANS WHO DO NOT fancy the idea of slavery must reckon with an uncomfortable truth: at no point in the entirety of the biblical canon is slavery condemned in plain, unequivocal terms. Sure, there's Exodus 21:16, which says that anyone who is caught stealing a man and selling him (human trafficking, in essence) should be put to death. But what about all the people who entered slavery to pay off debts? What about those who were born into slavery? Simply put, the Bible accepts slavery as a reality. If we were to look in the Bible's imaginary index for the phrase "abolition of slavery," there's a chance we'd end up pretty disappointed. There is a reason that many of the most ardent defenders of the practice of chattel slavery in the United States did so with a Bible clutched firmly in hand. It does not take a feat of theological prowess to construct a biblical defense of slavery. It just takes a desire to construct a biblical defense of slavery. This leads us to another foundational truth we have to confront:

Reading and interpreting the Bible often tells us more about ourselves than it tells us about God.

While it is an incontrovertible fact that many people who defended and benefited from the institution of chattel slavery in the United States pointed to the Bible for theological justification, it is also true that many abolitionists used the same Bible to defend their beliefs. I am not certain how much prowess was required of them to reach that conclusion. But I *do* know it took a great amount of courage to stand on the Bible when offering that opinion. Using scripture to demand an end to the status quo is rarely easy. If it were, then Jesus would have lived a much more comfortable life.

I'VE HEARD IT SAID that memory is the lowest form of intelligence. I'm not certain how fair that is. But I do know that I started reciting memory verses as a child. Before I understood what Bible verses really meant—or the circumstances under which they were composed, or how many times they'd been copied or translated—I was taught to memorize them. It started small. "For God so loved the world that he gave his one and only Son, that whoever believes in him shall not perish but have eternal life." (John 3:16, New International Version) Eventually we'd expand to longer chunks like Psalm 23 or the Lord's Prayer.

I remember vacation Bible school settings where we'd have to quote a Bible verse before getting in line to eat and the mad rush of hungry kids desperate to go first—because whoever got to go first always used John 11:35 ("Jesus wept"). I remember "sword drills," a game where someone would call out a Bible verse and initiate a race to see who could locate it in their Bible first. I do not look back on these times with shame or trauma. These are fond memories. But I cannot say they were indicative of any sort of understanding of the God spoken of in those scriptures.

We learned how to memorize without learning how to meditate.

Recalling the words of others has its rightful place in formation and development. But we are not growing in wisdom or authenticity until we've reflected on those words. We have to think our *own* thoughts about those words. We'll need to find places of both celebration *and* tension—of both affirmation *and* conviction—within these words for them to have any real impact on us. I don't know how to quantify the lowest form of intelligence, but I feel confident in asserting that memorization cannot be the sole nor primary means of formation and discipleship. *We need to meditate.*

I worry that many of us carry a superficial relationship with sacred texts. We can tell you what they *say*. We can even tell you what they *may* have meant. But I suspect that many of us mistake what it *meant* for what it *means*. Contrary to popular Christian opinion, words do not have static meanings. Don't believe me? "Awful" and "awesome" were once synonyms. They meant the same thing. Nowadays, "awful" almost always has a negative connotation. The pronunciation never changed. The verbal roots never changed. Yet, somewhere along the line, the message we received when we heard the word "awful" began to shift. This is relevant to us because the Bible is a verbal medium. Apart from some supernatural animation in which it hops up and begins miming, it can only communicate through words. And—if words changing meanings within their own language wasn't enough of an obstacle—the words that most of us read in our Bibles are *translations* of other words written in ancient languages of their own. What the words *meant* is (at best!) tangentially relevant to the lives we live today. What they *meant* will help shed light on their context. Their context can help us interpret those words. What is most relevant to the lives we live today is on the other side of this interpretive exercise. It is what the words *mean* that sustains us.

Make no mistake, there are plenty of times when what the words *meant* and what the words *mean* will be the same. I'm not accusing God of "casting shifting shadows." I'm affirming the limitations of human language. Memorizing without meditation will familiarize us with the words. But we can memorize the whole canon without encountering the God behind them if we do not make a habit of meditating on the words.

Memorization has its place. It is a fine means of familiarizing ourselves with the reality of words. In memorizing, we can pick up on rhythms and cadences. Many people have carved out decent careers for themselves as performers on the strength of memorization alone.

Meditation is something different entirely. To meditate is to converse with the composer. Meditation is the process by which we contemplate enough to join in the project of composition. Memorization is following the sheet music the composer gives you. Meditation empowers you to riff without the notes being laid out for you while still remaining in harmony. It moves beyond detecting rhythms and cadences and enters a world of being able to craft your own work of the same genre. Meditation is an act of wisdom. It fundamentally changes our relationship with the words.

TRUE STORY: MY SON learned how to solve a Rubik's Cube by watching. It was a long, frustrating process for him, but he got it done. He'd keep stopping and pausing YouTube videos to study configurations and learn maneuvers. He would ask me questions about how to perform certain algorithms, twisting and turning the cube in his hands to try and get it to look like the ones closer to completion than he was.

My daughter got inspired and downloaded an app that solves Rubik's Cubes for you. You enter the configuration of the cube, and it tells you which sides to turn in which order until the whole thing is solved. It was a much quicker process.

When my son turned the videos off, he was still able to study the patterns and solve the cube without the help. When my daughter put the app down, it didn't go as well for her. He'd learned how to look at and solve a Rubik's Cube. She'd been relying on step-by-step instructions. They were dealing with the same material, but their relationship to it was different. His relationship left him able to solve the problems by recognizing the patterns and knowing what the end result ought to look like. Her relationship left her dependent on having her hand held throughout the entire process. I don't fault her for that. Sometimes it's nice to have your hand held through complicated situations.

I suspect a lot of us approach the Bible like my daughter approached the Rubik's Cube. We find it so intimidating that we want backup when we encounter it. I know I've done it. I've even googled "what does the Bible say about . . ." for more topics than I care to name right here. I've plugged all sorts of search queries into Bible software looking for a quick solution to a complex problem. I'd love it if a solid individual would go ahead and index the Bible and provide a mechanism by which I could name any problem and find the exact chapters and verses to solve it for me.

My daughter's good intentions were the same as her brother's. She wanted to solve the cube, so she sought a resource that would chart the course for her. But that resource would never truly help her solve a Rubik's Cube. It didn't help her meditate. Millions of people around the globe go to the Bible every day with pretty similar intentions: to see where God has been made manifest in history. But we have never all engaged with it in the same way. There have always been different ways of reading the Bible. I don't think leaning on it as the sort of resource that charts the course for us will ever help address life's problems as they arise. I do not believe the Bible was designed to be that sort of resource.

———

I'VE NEVER NEEDED TO read the Bible in order for me to desire good. If I'd never encountered the Bible, I would still be repulsed by what my ancestors endured on the plantations of the Caribbean and the southern United States. I do not need to visit the canon of scripture for permission to mourn. I am free to recognize abhorrent behavior apart from the stories of scripture.

There are some who point to the Bible as the source of morality. That statement is refuted by the arc of scripture. The Bible tells us that Adam and Eve sinned against God before there was any idea of a Bible. God hits the reset button on all of creation six chapters into the Bible because an entire generation of Bible-less people have committed themselves to wickedness. God moves on behalf of an oppressed Hebrew population in Egypt before the words of the covenant are given at Sinai. The Bible is not the source of morality. *God* is.

I do not look to the Bible for a warrant to condemn evil. We needn't be biblical scholars to understand evil. The only prerequisite is some construct of good. And I believe that construct comes from the Spirit of God. I consider it an act of great cowardice to remain planted in the status quo just because you haven't found the exact chapter and verse to direct you to do otherwise. Only the most deficient and diseased of imaginations would relegate us to worlds constrained by what the authors of our ancient, sacred texts were able to envision. I look to the Bible to situate myself among the people of God throughout history. I am comforted that many of the things that I feel today have been experienced and wrestled with for generations. I am not looking to the Bible for step-by-step instructions on how to live my life. I thumb through the pages of scriptures, pausing where I notice things outside of what I'd consider ordinary, and I meditate on how the lessons garnered from these writings could affect my life should I decide to make an adjustment.

Instead of a step-by-step guide, the Bible serves as a seasoned companion—one containing wisdom as old as the earth itself. I tangle with the Bible, seeing what guidance I can wring from its ancient pages. I recognize that understanding what the Bible *meant* is helpful, but that trying to discern what it *means* is far more relevant to the reality I've inherited. And this requires courage. It requires critical thinking. *It requires risk.* Because, at the end of the day, trying to discern what the

Bible *means* always leaves you susceptible to arriving at the wrong con-clusion. That's a frightening proposition.

Fear has this way of keeping us frozen in place. The fear of the places our meditation may lead us can leave us stranded in a land where mem-orization is the highest virtue. And, to that end, many people have expended a great deal of time and energy in trying to create this index for us. If you google the phrase "what does the Bible say about . . . " you'll find a plethora of words waiting to autocomplete the sentence. We've found ourselves in search of a Bible that solves the Rubik's Cube for us, instead of a Bible that teaches us to recognize the patterns that will slowly lead us to a more complete puzzle should we settle on a method.

Courageous thinking helps us to search for whatever life-giving eth-ics we may detect in the scriptures and wrestle with where the God behind those ethics might be directing us today. The words that pointed to wholeness yesterday may lead to a less perfect destination today. We will not grow in wisdom if "what does the Bible say about . . . " marks the end of our investigation. That is an appropriate question to *begin* an inquiry. But if we stop there, we may end up stuck in what the Bible *meant* without wrestling with what it *means*. We will not develop an ethic that suits the brand-new, never-before-seen moment we find our-selves in. We will find ourselves trapped in a classroom where memori-zation is the only rubric. In addition to "what does the Bible say about . . . " we must also ask, "and how is the Spirit of God directing me *today*?"

This is what theologizin' demands of us.

CAR MANUALS ARE HELPFUL. They will tell you what various warning lights mean. They can tell you where certain buttons and switches to initiate certain functions are located within the vehicle. But a car manual will never fix a car in need of attention. The car manual may be able to help you identify the check engine light. But it cannot check the engine. Should the check engine light come on, you will need to hook your car up to a computerized machine that can identify the issue that triggered the light. To fix that issue, you will need to consult someone with expertise and experience in fixing cars. The manual was never meant to be the only resource you'd need to keep your car running smoothly. It was always meant to be a partner and guide for people of various knowledge levels who still need to drive cars. If you want your car to operate well over an extended period of time, you will need to incorporate relationships and experiences beyond the manual.

At no point does the Bible ever recommend the services of a licensed therapist. It does tell us that there is safety in the multitude of counselors. It holds elders in high esteem. But it does not say we should go to therapy. Waiting for the Bible to give me permission to go to therapy could have robbed me of one of the greatest gifts I have ever given myself. I go to church every Sunday. I spend hours in the Bible every single week. I pray and meditate. Then I take my hind parts to therapy every few weeks.

Everything in scripture suggests to me that God is committed to our wholeness. Why, then, should I deprive myself of the services and expertise of one who has trained for the specific purpose of helping people navigate the ways of being that make them less whole? In going to therapy, I've come face-to-face with the ways of thinking that prevented me from showing up fully for my community and myself. I did not arrive at this place of healing by indexing the Bible. I found myself there by asking how God would direct me in this time.

The Bible is a wisdom book. It can help lead us to wisdom. But wisdom existed before the Bible. I do not believe the sole purpose of wisdom was to author the Bible. The Bible was always meant to be a partner and a guide for people of various knowledge levels who still need to live life. Therefore, we must cultivate lives that value the exercise of wisdom beyond the reach of memory verses. While this is almost never easy, it is always worth it.

There is still a benefit to memory verses. They can help ground us in the stories of the people who've come before us. They can point us to the well-worn paths that so many before us have relied upon. It is easier to maneuver through problems when we can recall some of the guide. Likewise, biblical scholarship is still a worthy pursuit. But the Bible is a *partner* in theologizin'. It is not the end of it. Thinking thoughts about God is a serious and complex endeavor. The Bible will help us. But if we cannot learn to think on our own—without merely parroting—then the thoughts that we think about God will *always* be too small.

3

In-House Discussions

A big chunk of the work I do is examining how we read the Bible. Because when we fail to examine that . . . we are harmful. And I think, a lot of times, we end up universalizing in-house discussions (particularly in the Gospels & epistles) in harmful ways.

I TRY TO KEEP BLACK People Business for Black people. It's safer that way. This ethic ain't designed to be exclusionary. It protects all parties involved.

There's a phrase, "All up in the Kool-Aid, don't know the flavor." If we keep Black People Business for Black people, we don't have to worry about people who don't know the flavor tryna mix the Kool-Aid. Leaving Black People Business to Black people helps non-Black people steer clear of the dreaded (accidental?) racisms we see a lot of when folks who might be better served by steering clear of Black People Business keep looking up and finding themselves deep in the belly of Black People Business.

When I talk about "Black People Business," I'm not speaking of Black-owned businesses—which everyone should find ways to support. I'm referring to those discussions that Black people have among themselves. Those debates where everything falls silent when anyone who's not Black decides to chime in before everyone either tries to awkwardly navigate around this unwelcome contribution or decides to roast the presumptuous soul with no mercy. You can typically recognize Black People Business when you see it, because it's actually pretty rare to find Black people freely existing and discussing things in spaces where we do not have to account for non-Black people trying to police our thoughts.

Any time you suspect you could be witnessing such a thing? You've probably stumbled on Black People Business.

Identities are powerful things. Historically speaking, "Black" people are a relatively new concept. Don't get me wrong, the many peoples we now designate as Black have existed for as long as we've recognized the diversity of humans. It is the idea that all of these various peoples are somehow the *same* that is the recent phenomenon.

In the United States, being Black is sort of complex. I capitalize the B in Black because, at this point, Black is essentially a default ethnic identity in the United States. Most of the Black people I know cannot tell you with any high degree of certainty which African people they are descended from. That's not an accident. During the period of chattel slavery in the Americas, enslaved Africans were deliberately separated from their kin. At almost every turn, the things that reminded them of home—of being a people—were stripped away from them. There was a reprogramming process through which wealthy people with eyes on more wealth tried to reshape many proud peoples (who came with their own languages, stories, values, and cultural orientations) into machines.

I am descended from those peoples. I have reason to assume that I am Igbo in origin, but I came by that information as a result of DNA testing. My parents did not pass down many stories of my ancestors to me. They could not pass on what they did not possess. They could not possess what was stolen from them.

From the ashes of these many peoples with their diverse histories and stories and cultural orientations, this newly invented people—Black people—have crafted a new identity. In claiming Blackness for ourselves,

we declare that we are more than the tragedies that have shaped our histories. As is the case with any people, we contain multitudes. Our stories
are pride, humility, joy, sorrow, tragedy, and triumph. Black People Business is important because it is here that we wrestle with our identity. It is
in Black People Business that we examine how our histories have shaped
our present. In Black People Business, we are able to imagine futures to
work toward.

Black People Business is a beautiful thing, and that is why I am so
protective of it. If you are not Black and are fortunate enough to become
privy to Black People Business at any level, appreciate what you have
witnessed. But be clear: Black People Business is not *for* you.

If we can understand this reality, it will change the way we approach
the Bible.

———————————

THE BIBLE WAS NOT written to us. This is evident in the language
the Bible uses. The Hebrew employed in the Bible is not the same
Hebrew that is spoken today in Israel. Nobody today speaks Koine
Greek. Many of the messages of the Bible may feel applicable to us, and
that is *good*. We do share a common humanity with people across the
ages. We face many of the same problems. But the authors of these scriptures did not send them to our mailbox.

It's impossible to miss this when we recognize the cultural assumptions the many writers of the Bible held. Whoever they had in mind
when they wrote what they wrote? It was *not* you. It was not me. If we
assume that someone was talking to us when they were not, the only
thing we can be assured of is miscommunication.

Allow me to lead us in a breath prayer for a moment.

Inhale: not every conversation is about me.

Exhale: there is beauty in communities defining themselves.

Imagine, if you will, a world in which distressed communities have to reckon with who they are in the wake of, in the midst of, or under the threat of national catastrophe. Their identities are perpetually under the threat of imperial conquests. Exile is almost always in the immediate past, the present, or the eminently near future. Their customs, languages, communities, and beliefs are under attack.

These communities have acknowledged the reality of the tragedies that mark their rich history. Being intimately familiar with life as aliens in a strange land, they struggle to redefine themselves in their contemporary circumstances. To make matters worse, the most powerful government on the face of the planet has exercised its privilege to contain the fullness of their expression. Being too much of themselves won't just get them ostracized; it could get them killed.

You might be imagining any number of colonized peoples right now. Among that great pantheon of colonized peoples throughout the ages, you will find the selfsame people for whom the scriptures were written.

———

I STARTED USING TWITTER in April 2009. As an eighteen-year-old freshman at the University of Miami who was mainly trying to keep in touch with the campus happenings and get news in real time, I recognized that I probably wasn't going to be putting my best foot forward on this microblogging site. Plus, Black Twitter was a cultural FORCE back then, and I wanted to be in the thick of it. So I blocked my mother the moment I discovered she was following me on the platform. Ain't no way in heaven or hell I was tryna hear that lady weigh in on what I was gettin' myself into in the Magic City. In general, I knew who I was talking to in that medium. It was *not* my mother.

A decade later, I was in a different place. With a wife and a family to take care of, I'd begun paying closer attention to the way the things I said might reflect on those closest to me. It's not so much that I began censoring myself; it's just that my concerns shifted as my station in life did. My mother wasn't blocked anymore. I was still mostly in Black People Business though.

In 2020, everything ground to a halt when the COVID-19 pandemic took the world by storm. Everything stopped *except* social media. Around this same time, a trio of murders took place that awakened the national conscience to the ever-present danger that institutionalized and internalized racism poses to our society in general—and to Black people specifically.

On February 23, 2020, a twenty-five-year-old Black man in Georgia named Ahmaud Arbery was jogging when he was tracked down by three white men who were suspicious of his mere presence. When he failed to comply with the investigation of three random white men vested with the power of whiteness, they shot and killed him. Three weeks later, on March 13, 2020, a twenty-six-year-old Black woman named Breonna Taylor was fatally shot when seven police officers forced entry into her apartment as part of an investigation and opened a barrage of gunfire. Two months later, on May 25, 2020, a forty-six-year-old man named George Floyd was murdered when a police officer pressed his knee into Floyd's neck for nearly ten minutes.

With all these Black folks dying, millions of Americans realized that race relations in this country were far worse off than we'd been willing to admit. The vaunted progress we'd celebrated since electing our nation's first Black president in 2008 seemed nothing more than a charade. Many well-meaning white people sought Black voices that might help them make sense of some of the dissonance they felt between the America they'd once imagined and the America that had been revealed to them more clearly with each drop of Black blood screaming out from the soil.

This search for Black voices changed my Twitter experience.

In the span of a few months, the same account I'd been using to play the dozens and joke with the small Black community at the University of Miami and a few hundred other people in Black Twitter was being followed by a few *thousand* people. And a lot of those people were not Black. They were white evangelicals and exvangelicals.

Now, I'm not scared of white people. But I like to keep Black People Business for Black people, and I couldn't trust thousands of people who did not know this about me to govern themselves accordingly. I wasn't interested in telling anybody *not* to listen in. But, as long as people who were not Black failed to understand that I was not speaking *to* them, there were going to be misunderstandings. People assumed that their experiences were starting points for interpreting my words. This assumption did not simply fail to consider that my own, equally valid experience was just as good a starting point. It missed the fact that my experience was the *correct* starting point for interpreting my words.

You cannot understand anything I am saying without first seeking to understand the world I am speaking to. There is a technicolored tapestry of concerns, relationships, assumptions, and expectations in the background of every message that I craft. If you are unfamiliar with the world that shapes my words, you will miss the mind behind my message.

When I was able to name this tension, I realized something about the Bible.

For centuries, people who were not situated anywhere near the original or intended audience of the Bible have centered themselves in the sacred story, existential wrestlings, and self-definition of another people. This is the root of a multitude of misunderstandings.

———

READING THE BIBLE WILL turn you into an anti-Semite if you're not careful. Within the pages of scripture we often find Jesus disagreeing with his contemporaries. This was as common among Jewish people of Jesus's time as it is among Jewish people today. People who understood Jesus's time and place far better than we do held different opinions on a number of things. One of the groups we find Jesus disagreeing with in scripture is the Pharisees.

The Pharisees were real people. Jesus found them to be valuable people, advising his followers to listen to the things they taught. The scriptures tell us that Jesus often found the practices of some Pharisees to be lacking in integrity. Hypocritical, even. In the time since Jesus walked the shores of Galilee, many Christians who desire to follow him have been using the word "pharisee" or "pharisaical" to describe certain undesirable people, attitudes, and postures. This is despite the fact that Jesus does not condemn all Pharisees, nor do the scriptures ever depict him using the label to describe anyone who was not a Pharisee behaving in a way he deemed hypocritical.

The Christian co-opting of the term "pharisee" in this way has caused a world of problems for many modern Jewish people who view the Pharisees as the forerunners of Rabbinic Judaism. With the existence of far more historical evidence highlighting the threat that Christians have posed to Jewish people than evidence of Jesus viewing Pharisees as condemnable on the whole, it would behoove Christians to resituate Jesus in his Jewish context before recklessly using his Jewish words. Through shoddy exegesis people have been using the words of the Bible to sanctify their bigotry.

If we do not sit with the reality that every single thing we read in the Bible was happening in a context far different from our own, we are likely to use our own experiences as the most valid starting point for interpreting the words we come across.

If we understand "salvation" as something God does for us on an individual basis when we "invite Jesus into our hearts," then we may miss the opportunity to consider that the people Jesus ministered to were searching for something quite different. There is not much evidence to suggest that people were looking for relief from the guilt that accompanies using profanity. What we do find is desperate people living under the burden of an empire and clamoring for some sense of self-definition and wholeness.

I sometimes wonder if Christians would include the Hebrew scriptures in our canon if it did not point toward a prouder time in the story of Israel. If the Tanakh—the collection of teachings, stories, histories, and writing composing the Hebrew Bible—did not tell us of kings and military victories, how much utility would people who have come to revere the God of Abraham, Isaac, and Jacob *outside* of the law of Moses find in these ancient scriptures? Regardless of whatever Christians intended to accomplish by including these Hebrew scriptures in our canon, their inclusion does help us reflect on what "salvation" for the children of Israel may have looked like in their imagination.

When you believe that God has called you to wholeness, being subjugated is hell.

If you miss the power dynamics involved in crafting these sacred texts, you've missed the plot entirely. Many of us think we understand, and so we appropriate the stories of the people of the book and try to cast the roles with people we come across in our own day. This is most evident when we do things like refer to someone as a "pharisee" or describe their behavior as "pharisaical." This is easy to do when we think we understand the fullness of a disagreement. When we assume that our own experience is the best starting point for interpreting the words of a different people, we rob those people of self-definition. We have dehumanized them. It is *us* they need salvation from. *We* are the sin that enslaves them.

When Black people are trying to work out what liberation, self-definition, and salvation look like for us, there are disagreements. Malcolm X once referred to the Rev. Dr. Martin Luther King Jr. as "Rev. Chicken

Wing." Black men who appear to be especially interested in placating white people are often referred to as "Uncle Toms." Whether or not these tactics are fair is immaterial to the discussion. What is relevant for us today is that these are discussions and concerns that are held among Black people. If you are *not* Black and refer to a Black person as "Rev. Chicken Wing" or "Uncle Tom," you've just committed a racism. Those judgments are simply not yours to make. Those are in-house discussions. You are in the standing section. We can't even hear you in the house.

Is there valuable information for non-Black people to take back to their communities regarding the conversations *about* Black people that happen *among* Black people? Surely. Calling someone an "Uncle Tom" is an accusation that a person is so obsessed with advancement through assimilation that they cannot be trusted to protect the interests of the people who've sustained them to this point. It is a commentary on betrayal. Betrayal is a universal language. It can be communicated without calling someone an Uncle Tom. If you are not Black, you'd better find some other way to communicate that principle.

In the same way, there is no reason for anyone who is not Jewish to refer to anyone who has not identified as a pharisee as "a pharisee." There is no reason to refer to any behavior as "pharisaical" when what you mean is "hypocritical," particularly when there are plenty of examples of hypocrisy in your own tradition.

It is important to remember that Jesus was not a Christian. Jesus was born a Jewish baby and circumcised on the eighth day of his life. Jesus lived his life as a Jewish person. Jesus was crucified as a Jewish man, buried as a Jewish man, and rose from the dead as a Jewish man. Any disagreements he had with Jewish people about the self-definition, liberation, and salvation of Jewish people happened between Jewish people. Those were in-house discussions. If you are not Jewish and are fortunate enough to become privy to the rich history of Judaism at any level, appreciate what you have witnessed. But be clear: Jewish business is not *for* you.

If we can understand this reality, it will change the way we approach the Bible.

Like betrayal, truth is also a universal language. That which rings true draws those who cherish truth into the fold. When we see a Jewish man criticizing his contemporaries with many of the same criticisms we would levy against our own contemporaries, we recognize truth. Truth feels safe to repeat. And truth *is* safe to repeat . . . *if* we learn how to do it properly. In-house discussions only work if there is a reasonable expectation that the discussion is a safe space for transparency. If we believe that our words will be divorced from their original context and rebroadcast, we are much less likely to be transparent. We will not speak truth where integrity is not valued.

Jesus critiqued his contemporaries because, despite their many differences, they shared plenty in common. They shared many values, hopes, and communities. Unless we understand their shared values, hopes, and communities, his words become weapons by which we strip people of their right to self-definition, liberation, and salvation. We've turned the words of Jesus into weapons of mass dehumanization. His words have become our sin.

———

WHAT YOU CALL ME depends on who you are to me. There is one person on the planet who calls me Babe. There are three people on the planet who call me Daddy. There are a handful of people who call me Amandla—a Zulu word meaning "power" and my given middle name—walking this earth. Most people call me Trey. And absolutely no one who knows me on any personal level calls me by my first name unless they wanna make me cuss. The words people use to summon my attention differ based on how we've come into relationship. But relationship remains essential.

The key to understanding lies in relationship.

A central claim of the Christian faith (in just about all of its many expressions) is that God took on human form in the person of Jesus Christ so that salvation might be made known intimately. In order to *save* humanity, God *put on* humanity. In order to *restore* community, God *entered* community. The Divinity of Christ is incarnational. It is God wrapped in flesh. The relationship is the foundation of the words. The words are the foundation of the relationship. Without the relationship, we cannot decipher the words. Without the words, we cannot decipher the relationship.

It's important to sit with the significance of words and how they are received by different communities. It is no small thing that the outpouring of the Holy Spirit recorded in the second chapter of the Acts of the Apostles results in the followers of Jesus presenting the story of Jesus in languages they had not yet known. The Spirit of God is not concerned with all of us speaking the same language. Instead, the Spirit chooses to make those who took part in the in-house discussion capable of speaking truths in languages that define the world outside of the house.

The Spirit does not make those of us who dwell outside of the house speak the same language as those inside of the house. It is the sheer power of God that allows us to hear the same truth in language that we can understand. We can speak the truth without dehumanizing others when we listen to these in-house discussions through the power of the Holy Spirit.

Listening to in-house discussions is a privilege. We are not owed admission to the intimate workings of a people. When new communities of Jewish people *and* Gentile peoples form, it is not the erasure of Jewish nor Gentile identity. It is the realization of God's commitment to the wholeness of all peoples. Therefore, the ability to recognize the truth in someone else's in-house discussion and translate it to the vernacular of your own context is the work of the Spirit strengthening an ever-expanding community of diverse peoples. That is where the work of God is made known: in the self-definition, liberation, and salvation of a people in words they can relate to.

4

There Is an Ark in Kentucky

If you be goin' to Ken Ham museums, don't be in no hurry to tell nobody to "wait for the facts." You sit this one out, beloved.

"WAIT FOR THE FACTS!"
 I have heard this refrain more times than I care to count. With each Black body slain by sworn officers of the law—and sometimes even unsworn vigilantes—we grow angrier with the way things are. Justice organizations, activists, ministers—and whoever else is just plain sick of the same ol' same ol'—join a swelling chorus of *enough is enough*! And then there are those who are not sure if we've had enough. They caution against being "reactionary" and advise patience while we "let the process play out." It makes sense. The system was *designed* to serve their forefathers well. We tend to trust that which has made us whole.

 It was Tyre Nichols this time. A twenty-nine-year-old Black man who was beaten by five officers—Black ones this time!—from the Memphis Police Department following a traffic stop on January 7, 2023. He was taken to the hospital in critical condition where he died three days later. Following an atypically swift process, the officers were all fired and charged with second-degree murder just two weeks after Nichols's death. Video footage was said to have been as brutal as the infamous Rodney King beating that took place in Los Angeles more than thirty years earlier.

I am taking that on hearsay. I do not like to watch recordings of people being brutalized. It does something irreparable to the human psyche.

Even with *all* of this evidence, there were some people who were not yet convinced. They wanted to wait for *more* facts. There had to be *something* we weren't understanding. Everything would make more sense if we'd just *wait for the facts*. We had to see *the whole picture*.

I saw someone making such a case on Twitter. I was not surprised. That case gets made any time the police end up killing someone. I don't typically engage with people making that case. I get where their patience comes from. It is easy to be patient with a system that has historically served you well. However, one thing caught my eye about one particular person who made the case this time. They pleaded for patience in waiting for the facts . . . in *uncannily* close proximity to another tweet they'd sent about their experience at the Ark Encounter in Kentucky.

I *LOVE* THEME PARKS. Mostly because I'm a roller coaster fanatic. Still, the spectacle of a good amusement park? I'm not passing that up. I'm also a museum fan. My local library has a program where you can check out museum passes that typically admit four people to a museum. I'm a pro at scouting out when the good passes are about to become available and swooping in to grab them before the streets know what hit 'em. I'm not against attractions at all. In fact, I have some *dope* ideas for more parks and attractions we could use. Even Christian ones!

I think I could've saved the Holy Land Experience in Orlando, for example. In one of the most amusement-park-dense metropolises on the planet, the park where they reenacted the crucifixion of Jesus at 12:15 p.m. on a daily basis couldn't cut it. If they would've consulted me, it'd still be here. I'm sure of it. A thrill coaster called The Wrath of God. A virtual reality ride on tracks called 40 Days & 40 Nights. A log flume called The Great Flood. A wave pool with mini-ark floatables called The Red Sea. The Lazy Jordan River. A launch coaster called The Rapture. A drop ride called The Walls of Jericho. I'd have *crushed* it. I ain't got no qualms with a good attraction.

However, I question the ability of theme parks, attractions, and museums to fortify our faith. And that is precisely what the organization that built an ark in Kentucky purports to do. Answers in Genesis identifies itself as an apologetics ministry with the goal of helping Christians defend their faith and share the gospel. And one of the ways they do that is by building attractions in Kentucky. There's a Creation Museum and a big ol' boat built as close to the specs in the sixth chapter of Genesis as they could think of. There's a petting zoo. A restaurant. All sorts of stuff. By all accounts, it's really something to behold. A legitimate attraction. As an attraction aficionado, I can't even hate. Answers in Genesis knows how to do attractions. You'll have something to talk about.

As a minister, though, I do have some concerns.

I have been to "the Holy Land" (the one in Israel, not Orlando). I've seen the crowds at the Church of the Nativity in Bethlehem, built on top of the place where it is believed that Jesus was born. It is adorned with a beautiful ecclesial structure in the care of the Roman Catholic, Armenian Apostolic, and Greek Orthodox churches in what is now recognized as the West Bank. People from around the world line up to see the edifices and the birthplace of Jesus born to Mary. I have taken a boat ride on the Sea of Galilee, imagining the conversations that Jesus's followers have held on those same waters over the last two thousand years. I've toured excavation sites in Magdala and Capernaum. I have waded in the waters of the Jordan River. I've entered old Jerusalem through the Damascus Gate and bargained with the vendors in the Arabic market for trinkets and wares. I've placed my hand in the stone handprint at station 5 of the Via Dolorosa. I've sat in the Garden of Gethsemane. I've been in the garden tomb.

As far as Christian tourism passports go? Mine is not bare. But I am not sure how well any of those sights prepared me to defend my faith to other people. I did not fly halfway around the world to defend my faith to others. I flew halfway around the world to add depth and context to my faith.

If the objective is the defense of faith, it is fair to question what the *threat* is. We cannot defend something if we have not identified the threat. It seems the threat here is . . . well . . . people who aren't that concerned with whether the world was created in six literal twenty-four-hour days. The threat is people who aren't entirely convinced that a flood covered the entire face of the earth that we now recognize, and that the entire human species (and every other air-breathing species on the planet) was saved through one man and his wife and his three sons and their wives who brought a bunch of animals on a boat.

The threat is from the people who go to the Bible to mine for *truth* even as they are less concerned with whether everything in it is *fact*.

———

THERE IS A REASON we obsess over facts the way we do. Facts create the illusion of safety and certainty. When we "wait for the facts" surrounding the latest murder, we are reassured that things are working as they were designed to work. This ark in Kentucky? It's not *just* an attraction. It is a sanctuary, where pilgrims from all over can come and have the facts nursed back to full strength. This is largely because, somewhere along the line, some Christians decided they needed to draw a circle in the sand around the facts.

In 1978, hundreds of evangelical leaders convened in Chicago to articulate the doctrine of biblical inerrancy. They spoke conclusively and with certainty on matters of biblical interpretation throughout the ages. An examination of its over 300 signatories reveals that at least 95 percent of the people who signed the statement were white males. Do you have *any* idea how hard it is to gather 334 people in Chicago and have 95 *percent* of them be white males?

We cannot separate religion from politics. Religion is fundamentally sociological. Our religious beliefs articulate which stories, signs, symbols, and peoples we as social groups ascribe significance to.

Statements on "biblical inerrancy" do not happen in a vacuum. They happen when there is a concern that some people are ascribing significance to the wrong issues. It is no coincidence that around the same time that the social fabric of the United States began to disintegrate, a group with an *astonishingly* high proportion of white male representation gathered to set the record straight. The 1970s saw the anti-war, feminist, and Black Power movements in full swing. As subsequent statements on "biblical hermeneutics" and "biblical application" would demonstrate, the Chicago Statement was as much about restoring "order" as it was what the Bible actually said.

The truth of the matter is that the Bible is not as concerned with conveying *facts* as it is with communicating *truths*. If it were concerned with communicating *facts* clearly, we would probably be able to get past the second chapter of Genesis with a clear idea of the order of the creation of man, woman, and animals. But that is not the Bible we've received. Instead, we have a Bible that tells us that God is the Creator. If the Bible were that concerned with communicating *facts*, it might give us some idea of how the three twenty-four-hour periods were measured before a sun became visible on the fourth day. Instead, we have a Bible that tells us that the Creator was methodical and timely in shaping the world we now recognize.

We have a Bible that encourages—perhaps even *commands*—us to trust the God behind the text, even as we harbor questions of the text.

But when you are taught that certainty is the key to faith (and that facts are the path to certainty), you build arks in Kentucky to train people to defend their faith.

———

THERE IS HARM IN baptizing an interpretation of the Bible as "inerrant." It must first be acknowledged that interpretation is indeed what is being affirmed in such statements. We understand this on a fundamental level. The United States is governed by people who've sworn to uphold the Constitution. One of our three branches of government is dedicated to interpreting that document for us. We know that things need to be interpreted. We get how language works and shifts over time. The only thing people struggle to agree on is *whose* interpretation holds the most weight. In a fair world where community is valued, interpretations would be put in conversation. In a world where inequality passes for order (and order is valued over justice), one interpretation has to dominate the others. And so we call questions slippery slopes. We treat seekers as threats. We search for the facts that secure our position.

If we have appealed to one interpretation of the Bible as the justification for ordering our society as it has been ordered, that interpretation must be protected at all costs.

So we will sign the statements.

We will shame progress.

And we will build arks in Kentucky.

There is no harm in building attractions. Attractions can entertain and edify. But history shows us that there is great harm in misdirected faith. When you believe that the salvation of the world is bound up in the facts you've accumulated, those who've yet to come by those facts will look like demons to you.

The ark saved Noah and his family. The Bible tells us that it saved humanity and animal life as we know it. *But there is no salvation in the ark for you.* The facts of the ark will not save us. The poor will not receive good news from museum labels. Prisoners will not be released by animatronics in boats. Blind people will not have their sight restored by petting zoos in Kentucky. The oppressed will not be set free by the monuments we build to commemorate our facts. Because those facts will never feed our faith. It is by faith that the gospel transforms.

I DO NOT NEED to wait for the facts to be weary of people dying. I do not need the Bible's permission to lament another death gone viral.

There is a truth that transcends facts.

Facts are tricky things. They can be gathered and rearranged to tell stories. If you give me a palette of facts, I can paint you a beautiful portrait. But truth is the portrait we cannot change. I can slash at the truth with fact after fact, and it will remain unaltered. There is a Creator who deals in truths while leaving the facts for creation to sort through. The truth is that the Creator values the creation. So much so that the Creator marveled at the creation and called it good. I struggle to imagine that the Creator celebrates the monuments we build to facts while we wait for other facts to absolve us of blame for destroying the same creation that was described as *good*. The truth lies in our origins. God created good things. Facts can help show us where things went awry with those good things. But if there is any hope for our faith, it rests in the Creator of the good things and the goodness of creation.

Our doctrines are only as good as the fruit they produce. If our arks are safe havens for facts devoid of truth in pursuit of righteousness, the faith we are being prepared to defend is a withered one. If we are to defend a faith, let it be a faith in the One who stands in solidarity with the "least of these." Our faith ought to highlight the areas where the people that God called *good* cannot experience goodness because of our own apathy or antagonism. The truth is that we, as a society, have let these people down. We will not close the gap between anyone's calling and the reality they are currently experiencing by teaching them facts. It will require a commitment to embodying the truth.

Facts are not the enemy of truth. They are merely neutral building blocks. Facts can be used in service of the truth. But they can also be used to build a facade for lies. I can cite crime statistics or graduation rates that might suggest that some people are inferior to others. That suggestion would flatly contradict the truth of God. It is important to consider the structures we build with our facts.

Let us build monuments to truth.

Let me be clear—I do not hate that ark in Kentucky. I told you. I *love* me some attractions. What disheartens me is the illusion that attractions can fortify our faith. Jesus did not feed his disciples a healthy diet of facts. Jesus built faith through *stories*. Jesus invites his disciples to *experience* truth. The truth is embodied and lived, not merely memorized and argued.

A truth defined by the most privileged among us to the exclusion of "the least of these" will not reflect the fullness of the truth of the Creator. It will leave us bountiful in monuments but deprived of movements. It will lead us to certainty but separate us from experiences. It will leave us rich in facts, but poor in faith. It is not the truth at all.

If it does not set you free, it is but an attraction. A gathering place for amusement that is nothing more than an indulgence. A sanctuary of certainty. But the God of the Bible beckons the faithful to places where their certainty will not sustain them.

Abram's faith was recognized when he left the certainty of home and headed to a land he did not know. God led the Hebrews out of the home they knew in Egypt to inherit a promise in a different land, sustaining them with nothing but miracles along the way. With exile, colonization, and oppression staring the children of Israel down with geopolitical threats all around them, it was not the *facts* that defined them. It was their faith.

Depending on where you sit, facts can paint a rather bleak picture. Waiting for facts to make things prettier is a privilege I haven't been fortunate enough to enjoy too often.

But there is a truth that sustains me. I am not defined by the facts that people assign to me. I have been shaped by the truth of the One who created me. I have been created with the capacity to imagine realities that serve us better. I have the God-given ability to move toward a safer world before we have enough facts to comfort us in the unsafe hellscape we've made. By faith, I can summon a bit more of heaven on earth each day that I wake up. The same imagination that dreams of Wrath of God thrill coasters dreams of better tomorrows for the creation that made even God go *daaaaaang*.

And I don't need no ark in Kentucky to save that for me.

Part II

The White Man's Religion

5

We Don't Do That Here

There's a long history of Black Christians openly rejecting some aspects of white theology. Going back beyond the Civil Rights Movement. At least to enslavement and the second Great Awakening . . . possibly beyond then. Eurocentric "orthodoxy" does not have the monopoly on Christian thought.

I REMEMBER WHEN THE MOVIE *Black Panther* dropped. It was a cultural moment. In what could not have been a coincidence, its theatrical release fell during Black History Month. Black people hit the cinema in droves, ready to represent. It was hard to tell if we were going to the movies or coming to America. Some of us dressed like King Jaffe Joffer and Queen Aoleon. Some of us rocked Nigerian agbada. Some of us ain't go all out but threw on a Wakanda or Black Panther T-shirt just to let folks know we were there for the movie *and* the movement. It was gorgeous. For the next two hours and fifteen minutes, Ryan Coogler utilized the seemingly bottomless budget afforded him by Disney via their Marvel imprint to paint a picture of an African utopia.

It felt good to see a movie about dark-skinned peoples who were not enslaved. For two hours and fifteen minutes, we got to see a movie that did not reenact our dark past. We got to envision and celebrate a future of dignity and excellence.

Two months after *Black Panther* hit the theaters, Marvel cashed in at the box office again with *Avengers: Infinity War*. Entertaining as they may be, the plot of every Avengers movie is basically the same: the world is in grave danger, and we gotta get the baddest folks to ever walk this planet (and even a few other ones) to come and save us. But this one was different. King T'Challa, the Black Panther, done put Wakanda on the map. They get caught in the crosshairs of a battle they'd typically stay out of. The Avengers must make a stop by Wakanda for some reinforcements.

There's this scene where a few of the Avengers land in Wakanda and hop off their fancy little jet thingy. Dr. Bruce Banner (he's not Hulked up at this moment) takes in the amazing sights. He can barely believe his eyes. He asks Colonel James Rhodes if he's supposed to bow in T'Challa's presence. Rhodes sets him up to play the fool. "Yeah, he's a king." So when Dr. Banner sees T'Challa? He bows. Rhodes has his laugh. "What are you doing?!" King T'Challa has to set the record straight. "We don't do that here."

Royalty moved different in Wakanda. The customs everyone was familiar with would not suffice in this African utopia. What signified dignity and respect in the contexts Dr. Banner was familiar with was laughable in this new place. If Banner was gonna find any comfort in Wakanda, he had to learn to show up differently.

I REMEMBER THE FIRST time I saw a Black minister preach at the chapel service of my Episcopalian school. But let me back up a minute.

My parents raised their children Black on purpose. They made sure we held no shame in being Black. I grew up in Black neighborhoods. Clinton Hill in Brooklyn, before gentrification came and changed things. Jamaica, Queens. The south side and east end of Richmond. I had Black neighbors. We went to Black churches. We celebrated Kwanzaa every single year growing up, lighting the candles of the kinara and reciting the Nguzo Saba each evening. My mother took great pleasure in hosting our extended family and community each New Year's Day. A lot of people came because after all the work we'd put into our church's New Year's Eve service in the weeks leading up to that point, it was nice to kick back and chill for a bit. But make no mistake: In my mother's mind? That was a Kwanzaa celebration. I come from Black *and proud* stock.

I even went to Black schools. At least I *started* in Black schools. Somewhere along the way, my mother made the decision a lot of parents in her situation make. As she grew uneasy with the limitations of our local public school, she decided it was time to look elsewhere. My mom is a lifelong educator. She didn't take this decision lightly. She swung for the fences. Somehow, she got me admitted and enrolled in one of the most highly esteemed private religious schools in the region. And if you know anything about how these things tend to work? That school was *not* Black. At all. Since there were only eighty students in my graduating class, I could count the number of Black classmates on one hand. You wanna talk about culture shock? Imagine leaving a neighborhood where the only non-Black family owned the Chinese restaurant up the street and heading to a school where I couldn't blend in if I wanted to. Every. Single. Day.

So imagine my surprise as I walked into one of the weekly chapel services and saw a Black preacher waiting to speak to us. He dang near doubled the Black population in the room. And he got up and spoke *like a Black preacher.* He was poetic. Emotive. His delivery was equal parts rhythmic and melodic. I finally felt at home sitting in one of these white Episcopalian services. And I know this because I started talking back. I let a clap and a "Preach!" leak out before I came back to earth with the recollection that I was *not* in my home church. In this chapel service, we did *not* do that. After all those years my parents spent raising me Black and proud? I'm sorry to say I felt a little bit of shame in that moment.

WE DO OURSELVES A great disservice when we ignore the rich differences in culture that exist. Even intra-racially, there exists a multitude of ways of life. We do not become respecters of individuals when we rob them of the contexts they come from. We become agents of empire, whitewashing the things that make us interesting in order to construct one homogeneous whole. To presume that everyone who calls themselves a Christian sees, experiences, and processes the world the same way is to ignore the testimony of those who have come to experience Jesus *in spite of* Christians.

Howard Thurman talks about the role his grandmother, Nancy Ambrose, played in his spiritual formation. Born into slavery in Florida, Ambrose was deeply committed to her Christian faith. But she was not ignorant of the tension this created with her humanity. She recognized that much of what she heard on the things of God was presented to her by people who had no interest in seeing her free and whole. They'd used her faith as an instrument of bondage. Eventually, slavery was outlawed in the United States (except as punishment for a crime), and Ambrose would experience some notion of freedom. And in her freedom, she decided not to return to the land of her spiritual bondage. As her bright grandson read the Bible to her, she refused to let him read anything from the Pauline corpus to her. Those were the passages they'd used to justify dehumanizing her. These are the lessons Howard Thurman received in his spiritual formation.

Thurman went on to become an author, theologian, pastor, and civil rights leader. His seminal work, *Jesus and the Disinherited*, would inspire another civil rights leader by the name of Martin Luther King Jr. It would inspire much of what is now known as the Montgomery Bus Boycott. There is a direct line between someone who refused to hear Paul read aloud in her presence and the toppling of systems that kept Black people from experiencing the fullness of life.

It would be a mistake to assume that the theological descendants of those chaplains of bondage—who read Paul's command for slaves to obey their masters to those in the furnace of slavery—are the theological kin of the descendants of those who refused to see their bondage as divinely ordained. The languages may be similar, but the dialects are quite different.

———

BEING A BLACK CHRISTIAN did not seem like an oddity to me. I knew there were Black people who were *not* Christians. I have known many of them intimately and can find them among my family—both biological and beyond. Still, the idea that being Black *and* Christian was a different experience than being a "regular" Christian never crossed my mind. Remember, my parents raised me Black *on purpose*. Being Black and Christian just felt normal. It was normal to go to church and find time to celebrate Black history and grieve over injustice toward Black people. We never stopped being people when we became Christians, so the idea that the concerns of Black people were somehow irrelevant to God was a foreign concept to me.

My mother may have been in the driver's seat the first time I went to school with white people, but the next culture shock in the halls of academia? That one was all me.

I'd just finished my bachelor's degree at the University of Miami. Already married with two children and a third on the way, I didn't have a ton of time to figure things out. We were active in the church, and I'd already been licensed for ministry. I sensed I had a future in the church, and so I enrolled in a distance learning program at a seminary in my home state of Virginia. I knew the school was (almost exclusively) evangelical and white in orientation, but that didn't bother me. I already knew how to go to school with white people. By this time, I was a pro at it.

But there was one thing I hadn't accounted for in my decision.

These white folks approached God waaay differently than I did. I began to question whether the churches I'd grown up in were broken. I *finally* wondered if being a Black Christian made me an oddity. But my parents raised me Black *on purpose,* and it would take more than a few years of seminary with white evangelicals to feel shame about things my parents were intentional in making me proud of.

This is not a story about how white evangelicalism made me lose myself. I learned enough from my father to recognize that schools (or even churches) do not get to define me, and I can leave whenever I want to. This is a story about dropping out of seminary. I couldn't make sense of spending time and money in an environment that would train and endorse me to serve a people I was not in community with. If I brought that kinda stuff back to my community? I would've deserved every name they would've been sure to call me.

I focused on serving in my local church. As much as I enjoy *thinking,* my religion has always been tied to *doing.* My beliefs are embodied.

As to how far the academic pursuit of theology went for me? The further I got from my first stint in seminary, the madder I got at what I'd subjected myself to. I felt foolish having thought that I could go just anywhere and be prepared to serve in any context. How could a school full of people who experienced life so differently than I did prepare me to serve well in a community of people who spoke the same dialect as me?

I am the descendant of those who abandoned the oppressive readings of scripture at their first taste of freedom. What did the descendants of those who read oppressively have to teach me? What should I have expected but a slow road back to the religion that stripped my ancestors of their humanity?

IT MAKES SENSE THAT Bruce Banner wanted to bow before T'Challa. Banner was an American. We ain't got no king here. Most of what we think of monarchies comes from period pieces on Netflix and royal weddings abroad. They be bowin' and stuff. The world of Wakanda hadn't entered Banner's imagination. Upon encountering the reality of Wakanda, he was unprepared for a different way of being.

A lot of people approach Christianity like Banner entered Wakanda. We are limited by what we've experienced. We do not imagine what we have not seen.

I found comfort in the realization that my Black-owned faith was not deficient. It was just *different*.

T'Challa was no less royal than any other king of Banner's imagination. It's just that the way that royalty was worn and honored in Wakanda was *different* from what Banner expected. It was different from what he was used to.

―――――――

HOWARD THURMAN'S GRANDMOTHER WAS not an anomaly. Ultimately, every person who handles scripture as a part of their faith journey must decide what significance they attribute to which interpretations of scripture. For a people whose story includes the gravest indignities imaginable, it is critical to examine the gospel they are receiving closely.

Any hermeneutical or interpretive lens that allows someone who has never been faced with the prospect of bondage to implore someone who is in bondage to accept their station ought to be rejected outright. But that is not what has happened in the theologies of much of the church in America.

Here is a sobering reality: entire denominations were founded with the express purpose of preserving the standing of those who traded human beings of African descent. Since slavery was ended—or rather, altered—by the Thirteenth Amendment, most of those denominations have either ceased to exist independently or otherwise reorganized and rebranded. Only one of them exists with the same name under which it was founded. The Southern Baptist Convention, the largest Protestant denomination in the United States as of this writing, was created to protect the interests of those who treated humans like cattle. Currently, apologies have been issued, but no reparations. The names of some of the slave-owning founders of the denomination are still honored in prominent places on the campus of their flagship seminary. The legacy of this theology of oppression lives on.

While many people now recognize the horrors that occurred in the institution of slavery in the United States, I lament the fact that the church misses so many opportunities to wrestle with some critical questions: How could the church be at the forefront of such horrible practices? How could ministers serve as chaplains for the Confederate army? How could people who profess to be defined by love speak to people in bondage and suggest that God wanted them there? I would love to grant the white evangelical church a monopoly on grappling with these issues, but the facts are that many other churches have been shaped by the same approaches to faith.

Yet there remains a people forged in the flames of a different fire. The chaplains of oppression would not have the final word. Those who heard the gospel of bondage and rejected it went on in search of good news. And they found it.

I GOT OUT OF my first seminary because I refused to bring Bruce Banner's theology into Wakanda. I could not imagine walking across that stage, getting back home, sharing all the things I learned, and being told *we don't do that here*. Nor could I imagine going back to the people I served and telling them they got everything wrong. To say that would be to concede that the theology of the descendants of the people who sanctified the enslavement of our ancestors was somehow superior to our theology.

That would require me spitting on the God-talk of Howard Thurman, who claimed that Jesus went out of his way to make a home among the dispossessed. To try to bring a foreign theology back home would be to punt on the dream of Martin Luther King Jr. My church took the Bible seriously, but we also took Black dignity seriously. We would not find freedom generated from the source of our bondage.

The theology that shaped me activated the imagination. It required an otherworldly belief that—somehow—the same God who heard the cries of the oppressed Hebrews in Egypt heard the cries of the oppressed Africans in the United States. It made a liar out of any minister who said God's desire for us is anything other than freedom. It gave my forebears the courage to hear certain teachings and confidently declare *we don't do that here*.

I could not find a home at my first seminary because their faith was fundamentally different from mine. The language was so similar I almost missed it. We talked about "salvation" and being "born again." But, being raised as I was, I never considered that we might be looking at things of faith differently. Almost everyone I'd grown up around experienced life as I did, even if we didn't hold the same faith expressions. Yes, I knew white *people*. I just never had a reason to know white *theology* before. Coming across it did not strengthen my faith because it made no room for my reality.

Perhaps there is another timeline in which I enroll in a conservative evangelical seminary and feel celebrated and valued—not for being a Black face in a white space—but for bringing the fullness of my experience with me. That is not my testimony. Instead, I concluded that the marketplace of Christian ideas was much larger than I'd previously known, but that some places would be less hospitable to the orientation of my tradition.

I consider myself fortunate. I have seen a similar story lead many different people in a different direction. Some of us are not given room to view our experiences and theologies as *different*. Not everyone got to grow up Black *on purpose*. Some of us internalize the culture shock we experience as *being deficient*.

But theologizin' bigger demands that we view our experiences as valid vehicles of truth. When we encounter a reality that does not match our own, we do not paint over the differences. We acknowledge them. We sit with them. And if they do not lead us to wholeness? We firmly declare that *we don't do that here*.

6

Straitjacket Faith

The biggest threat to the gospel is actually the straitjacket it wears when the empire tries to take it from the margins and give it back to 'em.

MY SECOND SERMON WAS the hardest.

My first sermon was plenty hard, but I don't really count it. I only had five minutes to prepare before I delivered it in front of a full congregation. Our pastor was away from us one Sunday morning, and we had arranged for a guest preacher to deliver a message that day. But he didn't come. No warning. No call. The brother just ain't show up.

The choir did their best to stall, hoping the minister was just running late. They'd exhausted just about every song in their repertoire before we had to make some executive decisions. I huddled with the choir director, and we decided they'd sing one more song while I figured out what I was gonna say to all these people who showed up to church expecting to hear *somebody* preach. I went into an office, opened up my Bible, and noticed some notes scribbled on the sixth chapter of Joshua. I closed my Bible, went to the front of the congregation, and spoke on "The Strength in Your Shout" for thirty minutes. Then I tried (and failed) to forget about everything I wished I'd done differently.

My second sermon? That one was planned. I had something to prove. I had to let folks know I was a preacher for real. I don't remember what I talked about. I don't remember the key scripture. I'm imagining the sermon probably wasn't that good. All I remember was the first feedback I got from my pastor after the service concluded.

"How do you think you did?" he asked.

"I did okay. I think I could've spent less time in my intro and a bit more time unpacking that one verse . . ."

"Alright," he replied. "First note: lose the suit. That's not you."

I was floored. I spent all that time trying to craft the perfect message, and the first thing my mentor noticed was what I was wearing. And I looked *good* too! He was right though. It wasn't me.

I was trying to fight David's battle wearing Saul's armor.

Some jeans (maybe even slacks if I was feeling fancy), a sleek shirt (might have a collar, might not), and a decent pair of kicks. *That's* me. That's who everyone in the church knew I was.

The moment I put that suit on that morning, I made the subconscious decision to be someone who was not me. The people of the congregation knew me well. They'd watched me grow from a curious young man to the novice minister who'd be speaking that morning. And I was still busy trying to be who I thought they *expected* me to be. I wasn't comfortable being who they knew I was.

I was doing what a whole lot of Christians do in front of other Christians who claim to worship an all-knowing, loving Creator. I let shame cover the image of God in me.

———

The gospel gotta be good news. More specifically, it has to be good news to people who been through some things. The message of Jesus brings joy to the poor, the captive, the blind, and the oppressed. That is not an idea generated by liberation theology. According to the testimony of Luke, that's Jesus in his own words. It's a bit curious that so much of what we hear from ministers of "the gospel" seems to bring comfort to the rich, the free, the fully-abled, and the powerful.

If you emphasize the same social aspects that Jesus said would define his ministry and his followers, you're liable to get tagged with an adjective.

You're a *liberal* now.

That's *liberation* theology.

You've gone *woke*.

The *social* gospel is a *false* gospel.

Those with the *true* gospel—who've done nothing but "stick to the gospel"—will try to usher you back to the safety of orthodoxy. Even if doing so restricts your freedom of movement. Even if it means putting your faith in a straitjacket.

As I was introduced to expressions of Christianity outside of my own tradition, I became more aware of what is commonly known as the "culture war." There are Christians who feel called to a conflict in which victory is only achieved when their values and beliefs dominate the cultural landscape.

Where faithfulness is exhibited through dominance, anything less than dominion is infidelity. There is a danger to establishing dominance, for dominance begets dominance. Culture wars create culture warriors. Plowshares are hammered into swords, and pruning hooks are fashioned into spears. The work of the gospel is undone when good news to the powerful comes at the expense of the powerless.

Speak too much of power dynamics and risk being labeled a Marxist.

―――――――

THE WORD WE TRANSLATE as "Christian" appears three times in the Bible. None of them have an inherently positive connotation. The word was used to describe those whose situation was so bleak that hope in the crucified Jesus seemed foolish. The label belonged to the heartbroken, yet *still* hopeful, few. It was not a descriptor of character, as so many of today's Christians seem to want it to be. It was an epithet directed toward a people who practiced a faith that seemed naive.

A curious thing happened to the word "Christian" in the centuries following the crucifixion of Jesus. It went from a label that was given to the devotees of a slain savior to a banner that was carried by the conquerors. Not conquerors in the *spiritual* sense, who'd overcome the trials and tribulations wrought by spiritual warfare. Conquerors in the *physical* sense, who'd overthrown national, cultural, and ethnic boundaries through political and violent warfare. Christianity became the license for "good" people to do *bad* things.

Christians got to plant flags and claim sites, cities, and nations for Christendom. Anyone who was not a Christian became an enemy. Under the threat of these Christians, the options were limited: fight back, join them, or get run over.

And *this* is the ethos that drives the crusaders of today's culture wars.

The DNA of domination is a great political strategy. It galvanizes many people who are attracted to power. In sanctifying the quest for dominion, it pacifies the conscience of the ambitious. It reorients the priorities of everyone baptized into Christendom.

But it will throw your faith into a straitjacket.

In its rawest form, faith has unlimited potential. Left to roam free, faith unleashes the imagination. Should you be bold enough to try it, faith will have you doin' wild things. Leaving the familiarity of home to pursue promise in a foreign land. Walkin' on water because you could've sworn you saw your teacher do the same. Faith will have you actin' different.

In the hands of the marginalized, faith heightens sensitivity to injustice. In the hands of the oppressed, faith motivates people to chase liberty. Faith is a balm to the heartbroken. To the needy, faith is the path to provision.

To the privileged, faith unbridled looks foolish. Untamed faith is a threat to the powerful. And so it must be tamed. The best way to conquer a people is to separate them from that which liberates them.

Separate a people from their land, and you control their autonomy. Separate a people from their family, and you control their community. Separate a people from their language, and you control their communication. Separate a people from their faith, and you control their imagination.

———

WHITE EVANGELICALISM IS AN easy target. The vast majority of the criticism it gets is well-founded and deserved. But I didn't grow up in white evangelicalism. I am a child of the Black Church. I'm talkin' choir two-stepping into the choir loft wearing robes that dang near touched the ground. White-gloved ushers passin' communion and offering trays. The Hammond B3 organ letting kids know when it was safe to wake up because the sermon was wrapping up. I've never even *considered* joining a white church.

But white evangelicalism does not have a monopoly on tamed faith.

Many of us with deep roots in the Black Church have been able to imagine freedom for Black people—largely due to the legacy of Martin Luther King Jr. and the Civil Rights Movement. Even as we recognize Black dignity as a part of God's plan for us, we often replicate many of the same patterns of marginalization against *other* people. Without even recognizing it, our faith has been baptized into the DNA of dominance and placed into a straitjacket, separating it from its transformational power.

The quest for domination would have no hope for completion if it was satisfied with shaping white evangelicalism in its own making. That is not how domination works. If domination is not total, it fails. It wants to claim all the churches, not just the white ones. Apart from an untamed faith, the only ways to survive a quest for dominance are to join it or to conquer the one determined to dominate.

This is not a new paradigm. It was the same paradigm that shaped the world of Jesus of Nazareth. In an environment where people desperately wanted to *stop* being dominated, Jesus claimed to have the way out. Many of his followers assumed it would be the way that made the most sense to them. That the conquerors would be conquered through the same means they used to establish their domination. After enough time in the school of hard knocks, sometimes we just want our time at the top.

Herein exists the paradox. In order to exert more control over others, we tighten the constraints around ourselves.

A world built on hierarchies will never know peace. The structures built by the conquerors will only generate more conquerors. Exchanging the possibility of faith for the certainty of domination limits the creativity bestowed upon us by God. That is *not* good news. It is the opposite of good news.

JESUS WAS NOT THE only person who claimed to bring glad tidings. Caesar offered his own version of good news. *Pax Romana.* Roman peace. Order and stability for the low price of imperialism and hegemonic power. *Lay down your culture, your autonomy, and your right to self-definition, and I will bless you with prosperity.* This stands in direct opposition to the glad tidings of Jesus. The Jewish man from Nazareth says *lay down the death-dealing ways of this world—the dehumanizing systems—and I will lead you to wholeness.*

Caesar's gospel binds nations. Jesus's gospel breaks chains.

If we are not careful, we can confuse the two.

Culture wars demand an enemy—someone to pose a threat worth standing against. Culture warriors have proven proficient in naming threats. Feminism, "the gay agenda," liberation theology, Marxism, and critical race theory are some of the many things that have been labeled "threats to the gospel." The idea of a threat to the gospel is strange. Jesus once proclaimed that the gates of hell would not prevail against his church. That does not sound like the talk of one whose gospel is easily threatened. Nevertheless, we've landed in a place where threats lurk around every corner.

Perhaps the gospel being advanced by these particular warriors does not belong to the One it's being pinned on.

THE GOOD NEWS OF Jesus belongs to those who need uplifting. This is not a controversial or Marxist idea. It is an idea that takes the story of Jesus seriously. But uplifting the downtrodden is *bad* news to those whose prosperity depends on the bad fortune of others.

The synoptic gospels all tell the story of Jesus's encounter with a wealthy young man who meets Jesus, asks about eternal life, and leaves dejected when he learns that his path to being like Jesus lies in getting rid of his many possessions. Bringing good news to people on Easy Street is tricky business. The unabridged good news might sound a bit disheartening to one who is not in need of it. So Jesus invites the residents of Easy Street to relocate. The road that Jesus travels is one of *voluntary* identification and relationship with the downtrodden. It is in this place of humility that faith—that *trust*—in a loving God finds its truest form.

The marginalized people of this world are the most capable of imagining a more inclusive world. The disabled community is best equipped to lead us to a more accessible world. Women are best equipped to lead us away from misogyny. The racialized among us are best equipped to author a world without white supremacy. Indigenous peoples can best help us reverse colonization. Queer people can best help us combat a number of phobias. Faith in what we have not seen—*yet still believe in*—is what drives us to envision better ways of showing up and take strides toward it.

That's *bad* news to those who *like* the ways we show up now.

The closer you get to the centers of power, the more attractive Caesar's gospel sounds to you. It does not require a conscious decision. A passive acceptance of the status quo will suffice. Before you know it, you've become a chaplain to an empire. Your gospel demands that people lay down their culture, autonomy, and right to self-definition. You coax them away from the gospel of Jesus, placing the imagination it gifted them in a straitjacket that prevents it from building anything worthy of hope.

If there is any threat to the gospel, it is restricting its ability to make all things new. The biggest threat to the gospel is repurposing it to *reinforce* the gates of hell on earth. And that is what Caesar's chaplains do in offering Pax Americana instead of the peace that surpasses all understanding.

NOW I UNDERSTAND THAT my pastor was actually not all that concerned with my fashion choice when I preached in a suit. The problem was not the suit. The problem was *why* I chose to wear the suit. Before I opened my mouth to speak a single word that morning, I chose to present myself in a way that would make "respectable" people comfortable, even if it was not the truest expression of myself. I was more concerned with making people comfortable than I was with pushing boundaries. Regardless of what I would end up saying from that pulpit, I had already embodied an attitude that stood in direct opposition to the way of Jesus the moment I decided to put on that suit.

I don't beat myself up for wearing that suit. I was doing what I thought I was supposed to do. Until I took that suit off, I had no idea my faith was wearing a straitjacket. I didn't know my faith was supposed to have so great a range of motion. That was a decade ago, and I'm *still* learning to work the kinks out. A lot of my sanctified imagination atrophied underneath that straitjacket.

There's only been one time since then that I've worn a suit to preach on Sunday morning. But this time, my reasoning was different. I didn't wear the suit to make anyone else comfortable. I wore it to make *myself* comfortable. I'd accepted an engagement to preach at a couple of churches a long way from home in a tradition quite different from my own. I had no idea how anyone would receive me, and I was prepared to feel like a fish out of water the entire time. But I was gon' be the best-dressed fish floppin' round if it happened. That's what freedom looked like to me in that moment. The ability to go somewhere unfamiliar and stand flat-footed with a lil' edge of humor—even if no one else understood.

Turns out I didn't end up feeling like a fish out of water. I felt like a dude who was finally comfortable in his own skin wherever he found himself. That's the power of untamed faith. Where comfort is the very air we breathe—and not a resource defined by scarcity—the gospel of Jesus has taken root.

Scarcity is the currency of domination. Without the concept of scarcity, the empire has no glad tidings to offer. When people act as agents of empire, there are no robes of righteousness to offer. Only straitjackets.

Theologizin' bigger pulls faith out of the straitjacket that constricts it. Small thoughts and small theologies will not lead a captive people to freedom. Faith feeds freedom. That truth drives the need to restrict the faith of the dominated. If you spend enough time being restrained, you'll forget what movement feels like.

Sometimes, all it takes to lose the straitjacket is someone telling you that *you don't have to wear that.* I'm thankful for the wise words of my mentor. *Lose the suit. That's not you.* Those words carry so much meaning when I reflect back on them.

You were created for freedom. God made you the way you are for a reason. Don't let someone else's expectations define your reality. Someone else's breakthrough might be locked up in your truest self.

Caesar's gospel will cramp your style. Jesus's good news will lift the weary head. A lot of work has gone into making the two of them sound the same, but we can distinguish between them if we pay close attention.

Caesar's gospel will reorient your desires. The glad tidings of empire will set you on a quest for power and domination. Conversions that set people on the path to cultural assimilation will confine your communities. Self-expression will lead you to shame. There will *always* be an outsider to fear. You will be trained to fight in a culture war of someone else's making. Your faith will be neutered and replaced with mimicry.

And the good news of the Jewish Nazarene will plead for you to leave that straitjacket behind. It will inspire you to dream dreams. Belonging will define your communities. Your truest self will ooze out of your every move. Perfect love—an unshakable commitment to wholeness—will cast out all fear. You will be trained to lead everyone you meet to liberation. And your faith might mess around and grow wings.

7

We Gotta Have a Talk about Deconstruction

We gotta have a talk about "deconstruction." A lot of y'all think you've left toxic Christianity behind . . . but you have not. You may have left the creeds behind . . . but this harmful way of being? In which you assume to have the world figured out? You took that with you.

AFTER GRADUATING FROM A college prep school that boasted that 100 percent of their graduates were accepted to college, I did what was expected of me. I went to college. Not because I was particularly sure of what I wanted to be in life. Sure, I knew I wanted to be *successful*. But I didn't have a particularly concrete idea of what success looked like. I just knew I needed to go to college to get there. And so, starting in the eleventh grade, I spent a bunch of time thinking about where I wanted to go to college, because that could set the trajectory for the rest of my life.

This message had been drilled into me since forever. My mom had more degrees than a thermometer. My dad was a brilliant man—but not much of a traditionalist. He was a high school dropout who eventually enrolled in Columbia University before dropping out of there too. I'm the youngest of three, and both of my big sisters went to college after they graduated high school. I knew what was expected of me.

Education fueled whatever vehicle I was supposed to take to the top—and *best believe* I was tryna make it to the top. Whatever investments I made would eventually pay off once I made it there. As a seventeen-year-old former aspiring rapper, I knew a thing or two about believing in your ability to make it to the top. Back when I was a fifteen-year-old aspiring rapper, that belief kept me going. I was a more mature young man of seventeen years now though. I knew I wasn't gonna make it as a rapper. If I was gonna make it to the top? I'd need college. And I was determined to make it.

When I made it, I'd be able to buy houses and cars and whatever else I needed to live a comfortable life. I didn't know the details, but I knew the broad brushstrokes. This was foolproof. I ain't have a single question about these beliefs.

Fast forward a decade and a half and a couple degrees later. I been to college. I struck out on my first attempt at buying a house because I had too many student loans. I'd hustled *backwards*.

I was convinced. Education might be important, but college? That mess was a scam.

I've told that to anyone who'd listen. As a youth pastor, I told kids straight up: college ain't for everybody. That didn't make me popular with the parents, many of whom taught their kids the same things my mother taught me about education. But I refused to have an audience of these young people without warning them of what I'd been through. They would pay a bunch of money—possibly going into significant debt—to get a piece of paper that might not make them *that* attractive on the job market. Their ticket to the top might actually put them on a train headed in the opposite direction!

THE LAST THING WE want to experience is harm. While most people recognize that hurt is an inevitable part of life, some pain hurts worse than others. There are certain people and places that we seek for healing, and when those people and places end up being the agents of harm? We feel betrayed.

Proximity is a diabolical thing to weaponize. As we grow closer to people, we become less guarded. Though we may recognize the vulnerability that accompanies that proximity, we come to trust people not to exploit that vulnerability. This trust and vulnerability is the essence of community. The betrayal of that trust is the undoing of community. The undoing of community is the sin of the world.

Some people come to an awakening. They realize the faith systems they've been reared in have not saved them from sin. Instead, their faith has baptized them into a worldview that traps them in sin. One thing they know for sure—after so much living in this faith—is that sin is *bad.* And so they look for a way out.

Some people have to leave their churches to find God.

People mean a lot of things when they talk about "deconstruction." In Christian spaces, a lot of people are speaking of the journey I've described above.

Is anything I've come to believe about God worth salvaging?

Is there any truth to this God at all?

Has the faith that was presented as beneficial to me led me to being harmful to my neighbors?

In one of its more popular usages, "deconstruction" refers to the journey of reexamining beliefs. The journey does not lead everyone to the same place. Some people remain committed to their faith, even as they express it differently and hold things with far less certainty. Some people leave their faith behind, accepting that life without is just fine and becoming agnostic. Some people disavow their faith loudly, becoming heralds of warning of the danger their faith presents to the world.

I don't assume anyone takes this journey lightly. For many people, deconstruction constitutes their first serious engagement with their faith. Many people have become experts in Bible trivia—and sometimes even systematic theologies—without having considered their faith from the lens of an outsider. The views of outsiders are much more difficult to ignore in a world being rapidly reshaped by technology. The deconstruction journey is much harder to avoid.

———

A LOT OF CONVERSATIONS about deconstruction in the Christian space center people who do not look like me. Their stories are different from mine. Their experiences with faith often feel foreign to me. This is not a value judgment. This is an observation.

I observe these things because white evangelicalism does not exist in a vacuum. Americans of all stripes must reckon with what white evangelicals think, feel, and believe in some capacity. Powerful white evangelicals have intentionally and successfully structured society to make it so. When there is a shift in the atmosphere of white evangelicals, we all feel the winds. It's always tough to distinguish between which is the dog and which is the tail.

It is not as though Black Christians from Black Church traditions do not come to reevaluate their faith at some point in the journey. It's just that the language—if there is any used at all—tends to be a bit different. Reevaluating faith has not always been viewed as a cause for concern in my tradition. It has often been seen as a prophetic practice of sorts. The version of Christianity that was presented to the enslaved Africans was often presented to keep them in chains. A reexamination of that faith to detect any vestiges of bondage has been an essential tool to the liberation of its adherents.

And so I listen in on these conversations about deconstruction with healthy doses of curiosity and humility. I am curious about the paths that people who experience Christianity in fundamentally different ways take to this point of reevaluation. I am humbled by the fact that we've come from such divergent points to sate ourselves at the same watering hole.

But we do not all leave the watering hole headed in the same direction.

I'M A PROVOCATEUR BY nature. Growth is an uncomfortable process, and I'm an impatient man. Sometimes I try to hurry the process along by planting thoughts that provoke people to reexamine things in ways that nudge them outside of their comfort zones. That's just how I roll.

On one such occasion, I fired off a relatively harmless one-liner on Twitter. *Ain't no capitalism in heaven.* I can always tell when I'm about to have a time on social media by the types of people I tick off. Venture capitalist Christians *obviously* ain't like that one. But there was one former Christian who pushed back in a response that included some allusion to a scripture he viewed as pro-capitalism, along with an *extremely* unflattering meme telling me exactly what he thought I should do to and with Jesus. Now, I ain't new to this—I'm true to this. This wasn't my first rodeo. You can't provoke a provocateur. I ignored the meme and replied that what he was pushing back on was a teaching of Jesus's that he didn't like—which is always fair—but not at all related to capitalism nor the theology of heaven. I thought that would be the end of that conversation. I was wrong. Buddy wanted a debate.

There's something you should know about me. I do not debate everyone who wants to debate me. All that college ain't get me to the top like I thought it would, but I do know a thing or two about a thing or two. Since all the things I know don't keep me warm at night, I allow them to keep me out of debates I don't feel like having. I let this gentle-man know that fact when I declined the invitation to debate. It was not received well at all.

Confused about who this person was and why they were so both-ered by my disinterest in a debate, I started investigating. He identified as a deconstructed, former "Bible-thumping" Christian with a Bible college degree who was now a humanist ex-Christian.

I was amused. Not because of where his deconstruction journey led him. But because he'd acted the *exact* same way toward me as the "Bible-thumping" Christians he seemed determined to warn everyone about. The air of superiority and certainty around his beliefs. The enti-tlement to my time and attention. The argumentative posture. All of those things were front and center in our interaction.

It made me wonder what the point of deconstruction was at all.

———

IF THERE IS ANY value in examining the nature and validity of our beliefs, the value lies in taking account of how those beliefs lead us to *act*. Beliefs are only as good as the behaviors they engender. How we show up in the world is a better indicator of our convictions than any creed could hope to be.

To deconstruct and disavow beliefs without altering behavior is an exercise in vanity. It is not *deconstruction* at all. It is merely remodeling. Barely even a renovation. A fresh coat of paint on the outside of the same house.

It is imperative that we take inventory of the baggage we bring with us on our journeys. If we are not careful, if we don't see just how essential this work is, we can drag harmful habits with us as we rid ourselves of harmful beliefs. We can become evangelists for the same sort of arro-gance, certainty, and condemnation on either side of a creed. This

arrogance keeps us tethered to the same mountain, restricting us to journeying in circles instead of pursuing community.

The same platforms—free of accountability—that plague the
churches many people seek refuge from exist on the other side of religion. I cannot speak to the validity of the beliefs that many of us wish to
shed. I *can* speak to the value of community and humility. If deconstruction does not engender an appreciation for *the other*, then you've merely
become a peddler of a different form of toxicity.

As far as I've observed, we do not come to question beliefs without
first becoming suspicious of the behavior of the believer. If the beliefs
shift while the behavior does not, we may have pinned the charges on the
wrong culprit.

———

I DON'T HATE HIGHER education. I hate young people being
exploited to sustain a complex that has not kept pace with the society it
purports to prepare them for. I am frustrated that, in a land where you
cannot buy a drink or smoke a cigarette until you are twenty-one years
of age, you can enlist in the armed forces at eighteen and sign a master
promissory note for five-figure student loans at seventeen. I do not like
that promise is dangled with a price tag far too high for adolescent brains
to comprehend.

However, I have recognized higher education to be a bit more complex than this. If I were to crusade relentlessly against higher education
just because it has put me and many people I know in positions that are
far less than the futures we once imagined for ourselves, I wouldn't be
too different from the people who worked so hard to tell me that it was
the *only* way to the top. The power of conviction does not lie within
higher education, nor does it lie in opposition to predatory lending.

The power of conviction is in *our stories*.

A deconstruction journey that does not account for the power of the story is a journey that will lead you from harmful arrogance to harmful arrogance.

———————

THE MAN WHO TRIED to debate me on social media had a story. Out of curiosity, I learned his story. He grew up in a fundamentalist, white evangelical Christian tradition quite different from my own. While both of our traditions respected the Bible as central to our faith, the emphases were expressed differently. In his tradition, the Bible was cited as an authority in order to keep people in line. In my tradition, the Bible is cited as an authority to affirm our dignity in the eyes and design of an almighty God. My tradition applauded graduating high school seniors and even awarded scholarships to many of them who went on to pursue degrees at well-known colleges. His tradition funneled him to an unaccredited Bible college whose degrees would not open many doors outside of his tradition. His posts revealed that his tradition trained him to hide his sexuality. And that was an understandable breaking point.

As I learned more, I felt sympathy for him. Being told that God will never accept you as you are—and that you are only as worthy as your usefulness to the same people who will not accept the real you—is dehumanizing. Breaking free of that teaching is an act of liberation. The problem was that he never bothered to learn *my* story.

Had he sought to sit with my story, he may have discovered that projecting his experience onto mine was a mistake. He could have discovered that the beliefs he grew up with were not the ones I grew up with. We could have commiserated with one another over the various ways we felt bamboozled by our respective experiences in education. We had plenty of notes to compare.

But he did not see me as a person with a story worth sitting with.

He saw me as a mission. A potential convert. Someone he needed to break down so that he could build me up in his own image. He even had a podcast and a treasure trove of memes he used to denigrate the people who did not share his beliefs. He was certain that he'd found the absolute truth, and *no one* would be able to stop him from sharing that truth. And so he became something of a leader in the deconstruction space. He was the spitting image of the same people of faith he'd run from. In his quest for liberation, he exchanged one straitjacket for another.

HOW WE PROCESS EXPERIENCES is just as important as the experiences themselves. If we encounter an experience and assume the paradigm we use to encounter it is the *only way* to have encountered it, we have robbed ourselves of a chance at community.

If I assume that my experience as a college graduate is the one that defines the experience of every other college graduate, I have robbed every other college graduate of the power of their own story. When we assume that the way we encountered faith is the *only way* to encounter faith, we dehumanize everyone else who has encountered it.

The many people who rightfully critique an arrogant church can embody the same arrogance even as they leave it. If your journey through deconstruction does not lead you to a place of valuing the experiences— *and the testimony of those experiences*—of others, you are practicing colonizing of a different sort. You remain confident that *your* way is the better way and that people would be better served by becoming more like you.

Liberation lies in the community of testimonies. It is not in shouting down the stories of others that we become more whole. It is in putting those stories in conversation. Not *debate*. Actual conversations for the sake of learning about our neighbors, not convincing nor converting them.

Reclaiming our own stories is a worthy pursuit. Yet, if we continue to ignore, trample, and marginalize the stories of others in the process, we haven't grown at all. We have only contorted ourselves to fit into a new space that prevents us from experiencing life in its fullest form.

There is a wholeness to be discovered along the journey of deconstruction. It is possible to find your truest self as we untangle the many cords of truths, half-truths, and untruths that bind us. But it is nearly impossible to know what we look like in solitude. Community is the gift that helps us see ourselves. We will never know authentic community without authentic sharing. The best tools of deconstruction are the narratives that demand that we look at things differently.

8

The Truth Gon' Set You Free

Christianity is bigger than white evangelicalism. I know that a lot of conservative evangelicalism is predicated around convincing you that it is the most valid and primary lens for viewing the world. But it is not. The Truth gon' set you free.

M Y WIFE AND I bought a used car once. It came with in-dash GPS navigation, and we felt as fancy as we wanted to. But it was a *used* car. The maps used antiquated DVD technology. As fast as Miami was developing, there were all sorts of new roads and addresses popping up every other day that our navigation system simply didn't know about. The only way to update this was to keep buying new DVDs. We drove in a lot of areas that *appeared* to be uncharted territory. Our own house wasn't even on our car's map.

We had this whole fancy-looking GPS built into the car that gave the illusion of situating us in our surroundings. It had a whole lot of stuff missing though.

The people who made the map DVDs based them off the roadways that existed when they were programming the DVDs. By the time they started selling the updates, the maps had already changed again.

The system that came with the car was not equipped to take us to the places we needed to go. It looked fine on the dashboard. And it worked fine, as long as wherever we were trying to go was in existence when the team in charge of building the system got to work. If it wasn't? We had to rely on other systems to get us there.

EVANGELICALISM IS A KNOWN quantity. That's no coincidence. It is a deliberately loud and intentionally known quantity. Two of the things that define evangelicalism as an expression of Christianity are activism and conversionism—meaning that evangelicals believe in trying to alter the culture and win more people to their cause.

White evangelical power brokers like Jerry Falwell (Sr. and Jr.) and Pat Robertson helped shape contemporary evangelical priorities. In a shrewd political move, they helped orient the Republican Party around white evangelical values—giving the white evangelical voting bloc a disproportionately powerful voice in electoral politics. I'm almost hatin'. If you can pull it off, that's a genius move.

All of these things were in full effect a cool decade and change before I—a man with a child old enough to drive—was born. There are *millions* of Americans, over a third of the population, who have never lived in an America where white evangelicals were not movers and shakers in the cultural landscape. That's not even including the many Americans who were alive to witness the rise of evangelical power.

It's easy to surmise that evangelicals are the vanguard of Christianity. It would seem that being a Christian in these United States requires some level of affirmation of—and participation in—the paradigm of evangelical Christianity. The largest Protestant denomination in the United States—the Southern Baptist Convention—is an overwhelmingly white, evangelical denomination.

But that's a limiting view of the lay of the land. It requires the use of incomplete maps. It misses the fact that white evangelicalism—especially as it pertains to political power—is a relatively *recent* development in the history of Christianity. It makes nothing of the rich diversity of Christian traditions. It doesn't even speak to the fact that there are more Roman Catholics in the United States than there are members of the largest Protestant denomination.

I'm under no illusions that all these traditions are inherently more liberating than the white evangelicalism that has constrained our religious imagination. But they are *different*, and those differences warrant thoughtful consideration and exploration.

RELIGION IS, AT ITS core, a cultural and social orientation. While many people prefer to engage their *spirituality* individually, *religion* is an inescapably communal endeavor.

Religion is the expression of the significance we ascribe to stories, symbols, and people. Though there are some who insist that "Christianity isn't a religion, it's a relationship," it's more than fair to say that the Christianity we recognize as a reality in the West is a religion. At least nominally speaking, it is a belief system oriented around the story and person of Jesus Christ.

It's also fair to point out that, on the micro level, *not all Christians are practicing the same religion.*

We don't all ascribe the same significance to the same stories. We have not all accepted the same views as truth. We're not all using the same GPS. The maps are *considerably* different.

MARTIN LUTHER KING JR. and Jerry Falwell Sr. were contemporaries, born in the American South only four years apart. It wouldn't take me too long to present profiles of them both that seem surprisingly congruent. They were both Baptist ministers who went on to become activists on the national stage. In absence of a fuller map, you might read these things and deduce that they believed many of the same things.

But they did not.

Though he would later go on to retract his segregationist views, Falwell cut his teeth championing the same racist policies that King spent his adult life fighting against. While King named racism, militarism, and materialism as the three evils that plagued our society, Falwell became a spokesperson for policies that either tolerated or celebrated all three. Looking down from thirty thousand feet, it would be easy to say that they were practitioners of the same religion. But when you zoom in, you can't help but notice the inescapable differences.

The Christianity of Falwell is the antithesis of the Christianity of King. In theory, they ascribed significance to the same Jesus and the same stories of the Bible. In practice, they learned *substantially* different lessons from that Jesus and those biblical stories. The Jesus of Jerry Falwell said that proclamation was the main goal. The Jesus of Martin Luther King Jr. told him the gospel needed demonstration to be effective.

If these two Baptist, activist ministers from the South appeared to be driving the same vehicle, it is clear they were using different maps to navigate.

———

A GREAT DEAL OF the dialogue around religion in this country revolves around Christianity in general and white evangelical Christianity in particular. Often, arguments against the idea of religion are constructed with white evangelical Christian orientations in mind. When we speak of people who do not conform to that paradigm, they are often treated as exceptions to a white evangelical norm. It does not have to be this way. It *shouldn't* be this way.

We center white evangelicalism at the expense of the faith of so many others.

Religious identification in the United States, and much of the West, is on the decline. As mentioned earlier, the fastest rising demographic in this regard is the "nones"—people with no particular religious identification. But that's not the case on a global scale. In fact, people around the world, mostly in what is commonly referred to as the Global South, are becoming *more* religious. At the same time that we are becoming less religious, many people around the world are doing the opposite. While there are plenty of hypotheses about this development, I cannot explain why that is. I am merely amazed by the fact *that* it is. It is one of those paradoxes that reminds me that *we are not the center of the world.*

That's a hard thing for an American to conceptualize. We've grown up hearing that we were born into the most powerful, bestest nation this planet has ever seen. Criticism of the United States is often described as unpatriotic and an ungrateful posture toward a nation that many view as the best of what the world has to offer. This isn't an accident. We teach students to recite the Pledge of Allegiance before we introduce them to US History. Most children in the United States have faced a flag, placed a hand over their hearts, and rehearsed their dedication to a country *hundreds* of times by the time they learn the names of the three branches of government.

The maps are hardwired into us. The idea that countries around the planet enjoy many of the same benefits that we do never made it into our positioning system. A suggestion that other countries might enjoy benefits to a greater degree than we do? Anathema. We are the *leaders of the free world*. It is an incredibly efficient way of fostering pride and dedication in the populace. It also has the unfortunate effect of numbing our curiosity. It does not encourage us to ask questions.

That we are the pinnacle of excellence is the rule before we've even wondered about the reason. We can figure out how and why everyone else lags behind us at a later time. That is the ethos of many Americans *and* the ethos of many Christians, evangelical or otherwise. At this intersection, we find a powerful voice with a blunted imagination.

When we consider anyone we cannot immediately identify with as somehow deficient, we put curiosity in a box. When we cage our curiosity, we rob ourselves of opportunities to explore if there are other fruitful ways of experiencing the world. When we cut off avenues of exploration, we are stuck with the maps they gave us with the system.

PEOPLE'S MINDS GO ALL sorts of places when I tell them I got my ears pierced in Africa.

I spent my teenage years doing what a lot of teenagers do: trying to push the boundaries of what their parents would allow. I wanted my ears pierced. My mother wasn't having it. I tried everything. Fabricated paperwork to lie about my age and more. I was beginning to think I might actually have to wait until I turned eighteen to do it. Whack.

When I was seventeen, my godparents gifted me with a trip to South Africa. It was one of those short-term mission trips I have complicated feelings about nowadays. I saw a lot of the rural places many people think of when they think of "Africa." But I spent most of my time in Johannesburg and Cape Town, the two largest cities in South Africa. I was in a mall in Johannesburg when I saw my golden opportunity. *I found a Claire's.* I walked in and asked to get my ears pierced, and they sat me down and did it. You can get your ears pierced without parental permission at sixteen years of age in South Africa. My mother ain't see it coming. Sent her baby to South Africa, and he came back disobedient as ever.

There were no huts involved. I didn't visit some remote village where they pierced my ear during some special ceremony. I got my ears pierced in the middle of a mall. Right next to a Gucci store.

I learned a lot in that piercing chair. I learned that South Africa wasn't as different as it was in my imagination, but that it was every bit as different as I'd imagined. I spoke with everyone in that mall in English. But it was clear that English wasn't the only language they spoke. Claire's in South Africa looked pretty much the same as the ones in the United States do. But the rules were different. I experienced many of the same things, but I encountered them differently.

In the familiarity of home, I hadn't even considered that some countries might allow certain things before our age of majority. I even found out the drinking age there is lower than it is at home. I found myself wondering about the ways in which a seventeen-year-old Black boy like myself might encounter life in South Africa differently than I did in the United States. I had never thought about it before. But now I couldn't help but wonder. I saw that these people were out here enjoying many of the same things I did back home, but in fundamentally different ways.

THERE ARE SO MANY ways to love God.

A great deal of our spiritual formation is attributable to circumstances beyond our control. We have no say over where we're born. We don't get to pick who raised us. The maps in the GPS were handed to us. The first streets we traveled were designed without our input. None of us are formed in a vacuum. We are shaped by our experiences. We carry many of the lessons we come across—even some of the ones we'd rather leave behind. We are marked by our trauma. Our communities and families of origin have left their fingerprints at the core of our being.

With more experience comes greater understanding. We grow to understand that some people experience greater freedom than we did in our formative years. Many of us even decide to pursue and exercise that sort of autonomy. But learning to explore the fullness of freedom can be a difficult journey using outdated maps.

Sometimes, the best way to update the maps is through community. When we come in contact with people who were given different maps than us—who have been shaped by different experiences—putting our maps next to each other and examining them side by side can give us a fuller understanding of the areas we navigate.

In the world of God-talk, community can be the antidote to crafting a god in your own image. Allowing people from different cultures to converse as equals—not as deficient spectacles—grants us a different vantage point on many of the stories we've carried with the unspoken understanding that our view was *the* view. In trusting marginalized peoples to be reliable narrators of their own experiences, we learn more about what the love of God requires for "the least of these." Empowering women to lead, for example, puts a spotlight on all the barriers to freedom that men have put in place over the ages.

Inverting our interactions is a tried-and-true method of updating our maps. *De-centering* our own tradition as the most valid means of viewing the world gives us the opportunity to ask if someone else's insights might give us clearer vision.

I am a product of the Black Baptist Church. Though the Black Church is by no means a monolith, we are largely evangelical in our emphasis on the Bible, conversions, activism, and the cross. At the same time, I have learned so much about the many ways to love God from different traditions. I have gained an appreciation for contemplation and mysticism from more orthodox traditions. I've discovered the beauty of a more uniform liturgy in many of the "high church" traditions. I've marveled at the spontaneity of worship found in some charismatic settings and even in some congregational churches. I've spoken with passionate lovers of God in churches with formal, international hierarchies and in autonomous churches that started in living rooms. I've gleaned from people who love God but haven't found a home in anything we'd formally recognize as a church. I know people who love God but can't/won't call themselves Christians.

Looking at each other's maps helped us all become better navigators.

———

I AM NOT PREPARED to say there is no path to liberation that leads through white evangelical Christianity. I *am* firm in saying that no path to liberation will *lead to* white evangelical Christianity. There is no singular expression of religion that contains the fullness of liberation. Christians worship an indisputably Jewish man who never called himself a Christian.

We quote that man as saying, "Other sheep have I who are not of this fold." The people who walked the shores of Galilee, the roadways of Judea and Samaria, and the streets of Jerusalem with Jesus struggled to wrap their minds around the freedom he was leading them to. They too were given maps that differed from those outside of their community.

But there is life beyond the maps we've been given. There is a wide world of people on similar journeys who experience life in fundamentally different ways. What if some of those ways were capable of enriching our own experience?

The only options are bondage and freedom. Either we are bound to the maps that we've been given, or we are free to explore the paths our maps never showed us. If there is anything worthwhile, fruitful, or life-giving in the world beyond our maps, might that mean God has prepared more for us than we'd previously known?

Christians don't *have* to be known for wielding political clout. We don't have to be associated with patriotism or patriarchy. We don't need to be identified by loud proclamations that people struggle to reconcile with our behavior. These are all choices. But they are not the *only* choices. We can be known for humility and curiosity. We can be associated with friendship and our commitment to the wholeness and well-being of those we share space with. We are free to choose different ways of showing up.

There is liberation outside of the maps we've been given. The maps may have served us well for a time, yet promise often awaits us in unfamiliar places. God often draws the beloved into the unmapped wilderness where they learn more about themselves and the Divine. Maybe the people you find in the wilderness can help you find a way to pastures greener than you ever imagined. The only way to find out is by venturing beyond the streets outlined on the maps you were given.

Following the Truth where it leads may take you off the map, but it will always lead you to freedom.

Part III

A State of Confusion

9

The Church Gotta Pick One

The American Dream (preached by Democrats and Republicans alike) and the Age to Come (as preached by Jesus and his disciples) are two distinct, diametrically opposed ways of being. You cannot strive for both at the same time. The church gotta pick which one we preachin'.

I HAVE NO IDEA WHY I was in such a rush to be an adult. If I could go back in time and tell teenage Trey to chill out, I probably would. I think seventeen was just about the perfect age. Just before being of age with almost none of the legal responsibility. I could write a book on all of the responsibilities I hate about adulthood, but there is no competition for the top spot.

Cars. I detest them.

I don't like traffic. I hate gas stations. Renewing vehicle registration is like doing penance for a transgression no one explained to me. People expect you to wash this thing you *know* is about to get dirty again. And it's almost surely gonna rain right after you do end up washing your car.

Beyond all of that, car maintenance is the bane of my adult existence. If I had a single dollar for every time I took my car to get serviced for one thing and was handed a list of all of the *other* things I needed to address, I would almost have enough money to cover half of whatever I actually went to the mechanic to fix.

One time, I went in for what I was foolishly certain would be a minor fix and sat waiting patiently for my car back. While waiting, I noticed a sign on the wall. It read:

Fast, Cheap, Good. Pick two.

The implication was pretty clear. We tend to appreciate fast service. Most of us like saving money where we can. And we certainly don't enjoy paying for subpar work. But we don't get to have everything our way all the time. We shouldn't expect someone with the skill and ability to provide excellent service in a short amount of time not to charge us for their expertise and labor. We have to decide which path we'd like to pursue. Are we willing to pay the premium for the speed and quality we value? Or will we make a sacrifice somewhere to accommodate our financial situation?

Ultimately, we have to determine what we value most.

Many of us operate under the illusion that our civic commitments and our religious commitments are both guided by the teachings of Jesus. We believe that we have been born into traditions that have been shaped by the Bible in general, and the Gospels in particular. Given a pop quiz, we could probably provide some answer (if not a full-out proof text) to explain why we hold certain convictions, customs, stances, and ethics. We may even be convinced that our views are the way that they are because Jesus held these views.

A great deal of effort has been poured into forging these connections in our collective conscience. The Pledge of Allegiance mentions God, and the god imagined when those words are spoken is most often a Christian construct. The legal tender of the United States of America contains the phrase "In God we trust," a blatant faith declaration. It is easy to live a comfortable life in this country and feel no tension between your civic pride and your religious commitments. You can imagine them as one and the same.

But you cannot serve two masters.

The reign of God has not given birth to the rise of the West.

Here is one thing that every gospel account agrees on: Jesus died the death of an insurrectionist. Whether *you* view Jesus as an insurrectionist is irrelevant. The government sentenced Jesus to be executed using the same public spectacle visited on rebels in order to dissuade others from trying anything similar. If the way of Jesus was not at least a little subversive, it certainly gave the government the impression that it was. Wedding allegiance to the most powerful nation on the planet to faith in a crucified deity requires a gargantuan repurposing of one of the most captivating stories of the last two millennia.

When I do my theologizin'—my reflecting on the reality of God in our experience—I imagine a sign like the one hanging on the mechanic's wall. Except this one reads:

THE AMERICAN DREAM, THE WAY OF JESUS, INTEGRITY. PICK TWO.

THE SECRET TO AMERICAN progress is compromise with injustice. Our national mythology is riddled with contradictions. Freedom built on the back of the enslaved. Equality among the elite. The veneer of national pride covering the glaring national shame.

The only way to reconcile American history with American ideals is to start with an unrealized ideal and work our way backwards. We have to read our history through the lens of hope in these ideals in order for them to live on the same page. If someone from a non-Western context engaged our history without the biases we hold, it is not difficult to imagine they might bristle at the way that a nation built by Europeans and their descendants on non-European land treated anyone who was not European (and even some who were). In fact, you do not need to imagine any such thing. Many valid critiques of America's transgressions have been levied from people around the world and even marginalized people within America.

People tend to believe in America because we are *taught* to believe in America. This is not a critique. That would be a hypocritical criticism coming from a Christian minister. Many people believe in a Christian God because they are *taught* to believe in a Christian God. But belief in the progress and promise of the United States is no more natural or intuitive than belief in the God of Christian history. They are both generational constructs, built using stories, signs, and symbols passed down and reinforced over hundreds of years.

Understanding the process of constructing a belief does not render that belief false. Recognizing how we come to know things does not invalidate their truth claims. The only thing that renders something false is its incompatibility with the truth. And the truth is that compromise with injustice was an essential ingredient to the foundation and continued survival of the United States.

There would be no Union without the Three-Fifths Compromise, which originated in 1787 and allowed agrarian states with gargantuan enslaved populations to count sixty percent of their enslaved people in allotting congressional and electoral representation while granting zero percent of those enslaved peoples the right to vote. Compromises over the legality and humanity of chattel slavery held this nation together for nearly seventy-five years, before the bloodiest war in the history of this nation split the Union over the issue of slavery.

In the wake of the Civil War, there was more compromise over the right of the former enslavers to reshape the South according to their liking. These compromises put an end to Reconstruction, paving the way for the peaceful transition of power after the election of 1876. In order for us to move forward, the formerly enslaved Black people were left behind. The Freedmen's Bureau, established by the federal government in 1865 to assist the newly freed people in the South, came to an abrupt end after seven years. The price of peace was the protection of people.

When the choice was between honoring the humanity of the most vulnerable and preserving the power of the Union, the vulnerable lost in the compromise almost every time. That is the price of progress in the United States.

And that stands in direct opposition to the story of Jesus.

JESUS STANDS WITH THE marginalized and vulnerable. Every time. And on purpose.

The incarnation resonates because it requires the transcendent to take on the form of fragility. In Jesus, the indomitable chooses to put on vulnerability. The story of Jesus is one in which the power of God is not used to subdue but displayed in restraint and an unshakable commitment to the wholeness of those watching from outside of the centers of power.

The justice that Jesus practiced got him executed by the most powerful nation on the planet. The power that Jesus employs is not the domineering sort. Instead, the way of Jesus elevates humility and sacrificial love as the best embodiment of the power of God.

If we set aside ideals and sit with reality, Jesus and the United States define success in fundamentally different ways.

The United States has portrayed itself as the apex. It is wealth personified. The embodiment of power. If you let this country define itself, you'd never find a clearer picture of freedom—and much of that is because it is the pinnacle of power and wealth.

But Jesus says that true freedom is in *divesting* from earthly power and wealth. Time and again, the gospel suggests that the reign of God is an *inversion* of our earthly priorities. "The first shall be last. The last shall be first." If what America represents is the pinnacle of what success looks like here on earth, then it firmly exists as the polar opposite of God's reign.

Fundamentally speaking, the American Dream is a story of successfully navigating scarcity. Regardless of where you exist on the United States' bipartisan political spectrum, scarcity is a given. What is typically in question is how to steward the limited resources that we have in a society that is (in part) defined by limited resources. Some people believe that creating too generous a safety net disincentivizes people from the type of drive that keeps us moving in the right direction. Other people believe that trusting the most successful among us to create the systems that will sustain the masses will only increase exploitation. The common thread is that we only have so much, and we need to figure out how to maximize it.

There is no scarcity in the reign of God.

The kingdom Jesus describes is one in which the needs of every single person have been met—not out of their own accomplishments or drive, but out of God's faithfulness.

The ethos we ascribe to the archetype of success in our society does not lead to rewards in the society of God. For this reason, Jesus once said that it would be easier for a camel to squeeze through the eye of a needle than for a rich man to enter the Kingdom of Heaven.

Winning in God's reign looks a whole lot like losing here on earth.

I WENT TO A Christian school for kindergarten. Each morning we would recite three pledges. We would pledge allegiance to the flag of the United States of America; we would pledge allegiance to the Christian flag; and we would pledge allegiance to the Bible. I was five years old, and I was completely incapable of reflecting on what allegiance to each of these would require or what the act of pledging allegiance signified.

I didn't have the tools necessary to reflect on why a Christian flag existed to begin with. It didn't strike me as odd that we would rehearse our allegiance to a nation our rapidly developing brains hadn't begun to understand. I was not curious about why someone thought it necessary to craft a Christian affirmation in the same pattern as a patriotic verse written to honor an imperial nation-state.

Before I was capable of reading the words of these pledges with any level of fluency myself, a link between patriotism and religious devotion had been forged in my malleable mind. I did not know enough about my faith or my nation to reflect on whether I could pledge allegiance to all of these things at the same time. I was never encouraged to reflect on these allegiances in the same settings in which I was expected to recite pledges to them. These decisions were made *for* me.

As I came to understand more about the values of my nation and the values of my faith, I recognized I'd have to make a decision of my own. I would need to decide whether my nation's shrewd stewardship of scarcity would shape my understanding of God's reign, or if I would allow my hope for God's reign to override my intuited understanding of scarcity.

Simply put: *would I pray in heaven as it is on earth, or on earth as it is in heaven?* If you don't look too closely, those might sound like the same thing. Before I took any course on biblical studies or church history, I'd pledged allegiance to a Christian flag and a Bible. Before I'd taken any courses on American history, I'd pledged allegiance to the flag of the United States of America. Before I knew how to think critically, I thought heaven was an *extension* of earth, and not the *remaking* of it.

I lost my capacity for sanctified imagination before I ever knew God created me for such a thing.

The path to reclaiming that which had been conditioned out of me before I got to my multiplication tables was complex and necessary. I had to trust my ancestors to be reliable narrators of their own experiences.

I imagine that the American Dream I was being trained to pursue seemed like more of a fantasy than a possibility to the many people that the author of the Declaration of Independence owned. American values were birthed in contradiction. Oppression was the midwife that delivered the ideals of American liberty. Financial prosperity was paid for with involuntary labor. People were willing to die for the right to build wealth off the strength of dehumanization. This, too, is the story of America.

To the disenfranchised, there is no "good news" in toiling for the liberty of your oppressor.

———

"I THANK GOD THAT I am a citizen of the greatest country in the history of the planet!"

The room was silent. I could tell that line typically got a big reaction in the audiences he was used to speaking in front of, but this guest preacher was pretty used to speaking in front of one kind of audience. If I were a gambling man, I'd put good money on an American flag occupying a place of honor in his church somewhere.

It wasn't an overtly offensive line. It wasn't heretical or blasphemous. It just sounded a little inaccurate in the room he happened to find himself in on that Sunday morning. It wasn't even a particularly radical or progressive church. It was a church full of people who could point to instances in their own histories where the United States had enslaved or disenfranchised their ancestors, or where US foreign policy had made life in their homelands worse in tangible ways. Singing the praises of America in that room distracted them from singing the praises of God.

As much as his denomination emphasized global missions, I wondered if he'd have felt comfortable echoing that sentiment in another country. I worried that the sentiment would go unvoiced but still find expression in trying to turn all of those mission fields into some version of the United States. I feared that his version of *on earth as it is in heaven* was more like *on earth as it is in these United States.*

I had a harder time celebrating missions after that moment.

At times, the church has defaulted to providing theological justification for the culture at large. That is not a uniquely American phenomenon. The Church of England exists, in part, because of a political disagreement with papal authority that prevented Henry VIII from doing as he desired. The church has often struggled over political power. It's often been easiest to just go along with whoever is in charge.

The institutional church has often enjoyed the benefits of empire.

It is possible to enjoy the rewards of empire and maintain your integrity as an institution. It is possible to embody the way of Jesus of Nazareth and maintain your integrity as a people. It is *not* possible to do both of those things at the same time. You can preach the way of Jesus and serve as reliable chaplains of an empire, but you will sacrifice your integrity in the process. If you keep integrity and choose the reign of God, you will forfeit a claim to the sort of power that is celebrated in empire. If you keep integrity and choose empire, then the way of Jesus and the reign of God become a bit of a stumbling block.

Theologizin' bigger can free you from some constraints, but it will require some choices.

The choice of the church—between *empire* and *kingdom*—will direct the imagination of the church. Will we be bound by the concept of scarcity? Or will we enter a reign in which five barley loaves and two fish are more than enough to feed a multitude for an afternoon? These are two *vastly* different ways of viewing the world. One of these ways accords with almost everything we've known and seen. Scarcity makes sense. It validates the principles of law and order that make us feel safe and civilized. But scarcity *always* creates losers. And Jesus stands with them. On purpose.

The other option is an invitation to imagine new ways of relating to each other. The reign of God is one in which all of the citizens of the kingdom rest assured that there is more than enough for everyone to thrive. Care for our neighbors is the highest expression of our love for God in this alternate reality. If that seems utopian, it's because we have never experienced such a reality. These are the ideals that the way of Jesus calls us to strive for.

And so the church must decide which future it will work toward: will it continue the sanctification of American empire that successfully navigates scarcity, or will it pray that scarcity might become fictionalized on earth as it is in heaven?

Integrity demands an answer. Our collective imagination depends on it. The world is watching.

10

I Think We Got Shame
Backwards

Sometimes? Shame is a healthy part of a society. When a society decides to look back on an event or reality with shame, it can prevent them from repeating shameful ways of being. America is largely shameless. But some of us need to sit with shame.

I USED TO WEAR SUSPENDERS to kindergarten. You couldn't tell me I wasn't a smooth criminal in them joints. We wore a uniform. Navy blue pants, a yellow button-down shirt, and a clip-on tie. But the pants wouldn't stay up for the life of me. I imagine you're wondering why I didn't wear a belt. If you're not, it's okay—because I was. When I asked my mother to jog my memory, she stated plainly, "Your little narrow behind defied the confines of a belt."

So, each weekday, I dressed my little narrow behind in those blue pants, that yellow top, my clip-on tie, and my suspenders, and I went to school. This was back before I knew people thought suspenders were nerdy, so I didn't think anything of it. I wasn't even trying to make a fashion statement. I was just putting on the clothes my mother laid out for me.

Pretty soon, other similarly narrow classmates started rockin' suspenders to school too. I was a trendsetter before I even knew it.

I found myself looking back at this memory with a light sense of embarrassment. I wanted to call kindergarten-Trey all sorts of dorks.

But then I asked myself: *Where did that sense of shame come from? Who told you that there was anything embarrassing about suspenders?* Somehow, something as trivial as how I held my pants up for 180 school days (over twenty-five years ago) had been associated with being *uncool* enough for me to be ashamed of it at some point much further down the line. I haven't worn suspenders or anything resembling them on a regular basis since that time, yet here I was—feeling some sort of way about it.

People carry shame about things far more serious. Some people are ashamed of having more month than money. Many of us carry insecurities about where we are in life in comparison to where we imagined we'd be by this point. There is a way of carrying shame that dehumanizes the holder. When we begin to understand certain conditions as character flaws, we will think less of ourselves than is warranted.

This is an unhealthy shame.

Ridding ourselves of unhealthy shame can be a lengthy process. It requires retraining the ways we think about ourselves. We might need therapists, friends, and entire networks of accountability to support us as we come into better ways of relating to our truest selves. And that is a worthy journey.

But not *all* shame is bad shame.

MY FATHER AND I share the same first and last name. Even if that weren't the case, I couldn't deny him if I wanted to. I've been hearing that I'm his spitting image for as long as I can remember. Even if I didn't *look* like him, I definitely *sound* like him. My voice is almost identical to his in tenor and, at times, cadence. I got many of my mannerisms from him, and, depending on who you ask, our personalities are even similar. One of the last conversations I remember having with him before he died when I was fourteen was about his performance as a father.

He explained how his father (who also shared our first and last name, hence me going by "Trey") wasn't the best as far as being a present father went. My father told me that his goal was to be a better father to me than his father was to him. He told me that, while he felt he'd done that, he didn't think he'd "gotten the ball as far as he wanted to." He got the ball to midfield. His dream was that, one day, I'd take it all the way to the end zone.

I think about that conversation all the time.

The last thing I want to do is fumble the ball as a dad. I feel like I would bring shame to my father's memory if I ended up doing worse than he did. On the occasions where I am less than patient and understanding with my children, I feel actual shame.

This feeling of accountability is a sign of a *healthy* shame. There is a shame that draws us toward better ways of showing up for the people around us. There is a shame that compels us to do right by our forebears. There is a shame that requires us to lay a solid foundation for the generations coming after us.

There is a *good* shame.

YOU CAN MAKE A lot of educated guesses about the opportunities and obstacles a person will face based on the zip code they were born in. It's not an entirely predictive indicator, but there is a correlation between the circumstances that shape our lives and the places we come from. The way that we view and encounter the world isn't so often shaped by how much money *we* make as it is by how much money *our parents* made. While we are beings with agency and autonomy, we were also born into situations that we did not choose.

Many of us carry a sense of shame about what we've inherited. Grief, for example, is the inheritance of many of our neighbors. Some people were born into generational poverty. Violence and death have scarred many memories. When things beyond our control become pathologized, we can internalize our grief about them as moral defects and feel shame about them.

Expectations are shame's plumb line. We feel shame when we sense that we are not measuring up to a standard. If you occupy a lower socioeconomic status than you'd like to, it is easy to be ashamed of not climbing your way to the rung you'd like to be on. We've failed to live up to an expectation. But discerning between *good* shame and *bad* shame is often a matter of interrogating where those expectations came from. *Who told you that you were supposed to climb this ladder, and do they have the relational capital with you to set expectations for you?*

Shame is found in falling short of realistic *and* unrealistic expectations. Communal expectations *and* individual expectations can both be sources of shame. Expectations are a good thing to have, and feeling shame can be a sign of healthy accountability. But learning to differentiate between accountability and abuse can be the difference between carrying good shame and carrying bad shame.

There is no accountability without love. That is called exploitation. There is no love without accountability. That is called enabling. When the expectations we carry are given to us by those set on exploiting us, falling short gives birth to bad shame. When enabling is the ethos of a community, the capacity for shame has been eliminated. *Devotion without accountability is shameless.*

When we are held accountable by those who love us, shame is an invitation to wholeness.

THERE WAS A TIME when I wasn't *anybody's* idea of a "good" person. I was kinda a jerk. I knew how to put a good face on, but I was a self-centered person. I was my number one priority, and I would not hesitate to prioritize myself at anyone else's expense. I don't just mean for survival, health, and wholeness either. I mean trivial stuff. I was gon' get mine.

When I look back on the person I used to be, I am ashamed. I am embarrassed by the way I used to behave. It was a poor reflection of the family I came from. It was an insult to that memorable conversation I had with my father. It would serve as an awful example for the children I'd eventually have one day. That person would have been a terrible partner to the woman who is now my wife. I was accountable to *no one*, which means I'd cut myself off from experiencing the love anyone may have desired to share with me.

Through some combination of immaturity and outright selfishness, I'd made up my mind that I would do what I wanted—regardless of how it impacted anyone else. The only way to get close to me was by enabling me to behave how I wanted. Paradoxically, the only way to get close to me was by putting yourself in harm's way. If love is a two-way street, that road was shut down both ways.

I am not proud of the person I used to be. Each day, I wake up determined not to behave like that person. Shame can be a powerful motivator.

This shame has not rendered me incapable of growth. It has liberated me from the captivity of a way of being that served no one well. This is a *good* shame.

WE HAVE A COMPLEX relationship with the word "shame" nowadays. Many have an equally complicated relationship with the word "religion." In fact, I've even heard a statement to the effect of, "religion puts shame *on* you, while relationship takes shame *off* you."

I suspect that negative feelings associated with the words "shame" and "religion" share the same source: accountability with no love. People run from shame and religion because both have become weapons of exploitation.

Religion, divorced from a true commitment to communal wholeness, has indeed been an incubator for negative sorts of shame. It is not difficult to trace the shame felt, or once felt, about bodies or sexuality or emotions or resentment back to the platitudes and attitudes we've inherited.

But shame *and* religion can both be redeemed when they are reestablished in community and guided by love.

When stewarded through community—as opposed to weaponized by communities—religion is fundamentally about the significance we ascribe to stories, signs, and symbols. There is nothing inherently bad about that. The stories that societies revere are often unique to those societies. They may not all be empirically factual according to our modern journalistic standards, but they all aim to communicate a truth that defines that culture.

There is no evidence that a young George Washington actually damaged his father's cherry tree with a hatchet, or that he uttered the famous "I cannot tell a lie" line when confessing to this transgression. Yet generations of children heard this story and accepted it as a truth about a founding father of the United States. The power of this story is not in the facts behind the events. The power of this story is in the truth that it communicates: that George Washington was a man of virtue who set a virtuous standard for all the many presidents that would come after him. A president who was less virtuous than he was could rightfully be shamed for not living up to a standard. The story—with its almost canonical status—communicates a virtue that sets a standard. That standard becomes a measuring stick which can be used to promote a healthy sense of shame.

But this analogy does fall apart, because George Washington was not merely a mythological figure. He was a human. A human who traded in Black bodies and was only virtuous by the newly burgeoning standards of whiteness. Exalting Washington as the standard by which virtue is measured actually heaps the *bad* kind of shame on the descendants of the people he once owned and brutalized. And that is backwards.

Imagine how our society might look today if we carried a sense of shame about the fact that our original standard-bearers for virtue still treated people like animals.

HEALTHY SHAME REQUIRES THAT we tell the whole truth. Not just the parts that make us proud.

We need to be honest about the ways we have failed to live up to our highest ideals. People cannot be judged by the standards of their own time at the same time they are held up as paragons of virtue for our own. That is an exercise in mythmaking, and myths without truth are just broken narratives that will never make one whole.

It is easy to desire to "make America great again" if you refuse to reckon with the ways that it has *consistently* failed to adequately and justly tend to the most vulnerable people of the land. Our shamelessness has led us to a pride that prevents us from becoming our best selves.

When you are the hero in every story, you have probably gotten shame wrong.

In this way, many Christians in Western settings (like the US) struggle to make sense of how to relate to shame. We recognize that shame and religion often go hand in hand. But we simply do not like shame. And so Christians are the good guys in all of our stories.

In the collective memory of Christians, we are the stewards of the arts and sciences. We are the custodians of virtue. We are the charitable. We are the keepers of morality.

Yes, Christians have also been the wagers of war, the enslavers and traders, and the theologians who have explained all of this away. But those are minor blemishes in a rather spotless record—according to our Christian imaginations.

It is good to celebrate our wins. But we will never grow if we do not learn to sit with the ways that we have fallen short of the best that we— as a people—are capable of.

HEALTHY SHAME MIGHT BE the surest path to humility, and humility is the only way to make sense of Jesus.

In the Gospels, Jesus is one who rescues people from *unhealthy* senses of shame. Jesus stands with a woman who was caught in the act of adultery, questioning who is qualified to accuse her of sin (and perhaps wondering why nobody bothered to accuse the man she was allegedly caught in the act with). Jesus heals people with ailments that place them on the margins of their community. Jesus dines with disreputable people and stands by these choices among the highly esteemed. Time and again, Jesus shows compassion to the shamed of society.

And time and again, Jesus shames the privileged of society. It is Jesus who notices that a widow who gave a little bit had actually given more than anyone else, to the shame of those who had more to give. Jesus grants the little children an audience while he shames his own disciples for trying to stand in their way. Jesus invites one of the convicts who was crucified with him into eternal paradise while shaming the free people who watched it all happen when he asked the Father to forgive them in their ignorance.

Jesus shames the powerful people who are used to doing the shaming while uplifting the same people the powerful usually shame.

Shame is how we level the playing field.

When we understand shame as a friend of the defenseless, we are on the path to wholeness.

Some things we ought to be ashamed of. We ought to be ashamed that many of the people whose labor we depend on to keep things running can barely afford to support themselves. We ought to be ashamed of the number of unhoused people who experience homelessness in one of the wealthiest nations in the history of the planet. We ought to be ashamed that children who are learning about themselves and the deeply complicated reality of human sexuality must navigate such a heavy anxiety as a direct result of our inability or lack of desire to walk with them safely through this journey. We ought to be ashamed that we demand better decorum of protestors than we do of our own elected officials.

Shame is an invitation to do better by our neighbors.

Too often, shame is used as a weapon to club an already hurting people further into submission. When it's deployed often and effectively enough, we don't even have to wield the weapon anymore. People will use it on themselves. People whose greatest crime is being different in any way will end up confessing to crimes they have not committed because they already know how the trial goes. When we are guided by unhealthy shame, a jury of our peers will always find us guilty.

But when we understand shame as a means by which accountability—real accountability, grounded in love—is effected, we invite communities into wholeness. Shame becomes a path to confession, repentance, and repair.

"I am ashamed of the way I behaved. I now recognize that what I did was harmful. I am committed to being a better neighbor to you."

"We are ashamed of the way these things came to be. We now recognize that harmful patterns have been set in place. We are committed to being a safe community for you all."

If we are comfortable ascribing significance to the *whole truth*—and not just our unexamined stories—we can write new endings to these stories. Our communities can live into the promises we speak over them. We can learn to be trustworthy. Our neighbors can breathe more easily. Sitting with shame might be the only way for us to stand in freedom. We will not find wholeness by weaponizing shame against the vulnerable. We might find liberation by embracing shame as a society. Because there is no love without accountability.

11

I Got a Dope Résumé
for Grifting

*I have an impeccable résumé for Token Black Conservative Grifting! The
Black son of an immigrant with a degree from a PWI and a degree from an
HBCU and a code switcher I use so rarely it's still like new! I'm charging a
premium!*

I WAS A THEATER KID. International Thespian Society and all
that. I liked playing sports too, but after a back surgery sidelined me
for most of a year, I'd pretty much spent most of my extracurricular
hours on or near a stage.

I appreciated the agreement the audience had with us: *You can lie to
us, and we will let you. But you have to commit to doing it well.*

Suspension of disbelief. That's the name they give the principle that
describes this pact between actors, a crew, and an audience. That's how we
allow ourselves to enjoy all of the non-white people dancing, singing, and
rapping America into existence when we're watching *Hamilton*. It's how an
ensemble of entirely teenage actors can put on a production about married
couples with adult children. When we enter a theater, we are prepared to
abandon our logic. We've decided not to think too hard about that which
we know to be unreal.

The only way to enjoy the production is if we agree to suspend
disbelief.

Maybe this understanding is why I enjoyed pro wrestling so much when I was a kid. I knew the storylines were scripted. The match outcomes were determined long before the broadcast started. But there was still something mesmerizing about the choreographed athleticism. The violence was easier to stomach when I knew it was mapped out beforehand. It was the perfect marriage of the competitiveness of sports and the performances I'd come to appreciate on the stage.

But suspending your disbelief is typically relegated to *performances*. We are willing to be lied to when we understand that someone is pretending to be someone/something they are not. We do not often carry this same willingness into arenas where we expect people to show up authentically.

Belief is a vulnerable thing. What we believe can shape our actions, relationships, and destinies. In this way, *disbelief* often functions as a safety mechanism of sorts.

If you can bypass someone's disbelief, you can steer their imagination.

———

BELIEFS MARK THE BOUNDARIES of Christianity. From a cultural and functional standpoint, people are often *born into* Christianity. But the mere existence of "orthodoxy" and confessions suggest that, more than many other religious systems, Christianity is defined by *beliefs*. If you ask the average Western Christian about their journey in the land of Christian faith, I'd wager that you are more likely to hear about the process of adopting and developing a set of beliefs than you are to hear about how they found belonging in a particular community.

In an ideal world, we'd find belonging in communities grounded in belief. However, when beliefs become boundaries, you are just as likely to find yourself on the outside looking in at the first sign of divergence.

Show and *tell.* Those are the two ways to let someone know what you believe.

On one hand, you *show* people what you believe by the way you live. If you spend enough time with someone, you can pick up on the things they value. You'll learn about their principles and ethics. What is in and out of bounds for them becomes apparent. You can catch a lot by observing someone. Give it time. People will show you what they believe.

On the other hand, the Christianity so many of us know is a bit different. We allow people to *tell* us what they believe. Through professing a belief or conviction, people can situate themselves within a Christian boundary. The belief is the boundary, and—if you know how to communicate the belief proficiently—you can talk yourself into a lot of communities.

Showing is the more proven method of identifying a belief. But, nowadays, we allow a whole lot of telling to take its place. If you know the right things to say, you can give the *appearance* of showing when all you're really doing is telling. You can perform your way into a lot of Christian communities.

I DON'T KNOW HOW many of y'all would know me if it wasn't for Twitter. Even if you didn't first come across me there, you're probably not too many degrees of separation removed from somebody who found out about me on the app. I'm not sure if anyone would have had any interest in publishing any book of mine were it not for a decent-sized social media presence.

I spent a decade on Twitter just chillin'. The platform first got its legs under it when I was in college. Like I mentioned in chapter 3, I used it as a way to connect with my friends around campus and comment on things happening at our school, on TV, and in music. Black

Twitter was poppin'. That's where I spent most of my time. Even after I graduated.

Black Twitter was where I wanted to be.

Like a lot of people do between the ages of eighteen and thirty, I gradually changed. I wasn't a college kid anymore. I'd gotten married. Had children. I'd started a career. Begun a journey in ministry. My social media conduct changed a lot. My values were reflected in the things I shared. I chose a new Twitter handle to reflect my identity *and* my values. I was PastorTrey05, a hat tip to Atlanta rapper Pastor Troy, my new vocation in ministry, and the 305 area code of Miami-Dade County—where a lot of this began for me.

But I was still on Black Twitter.

And then 2020 happened, with the pandemic pushing a lot of people inside and online. Virtual meetings became fixtures, and a whole bunch of us started spending more time on the internet. While many of us were inside and online, the murders of Ahmaud Arbery, Breonna Taylor, and George Floyd pushed issues of systemic racism to the forefront of the national conversation. Sports franchises started painting anti-racist slogans on uniforms, courts, and fields—two of them even changed their names. Municipalities started painting "Black Lives Matter" on streets. Corporations were voicing commitments to racial justice.

And a whole lot of white Christians realized there was a whole lot of racism baked into their institutions and traditions.

Being online in this kind of climate made Black voices something of a commodity. I don't know how or when it happened, but—for the first time in my decade and change on that platform—white people found me. My follower count started to climb.

I was confronted with a choice. Would I continue being the same Trey I'd been up to that point? Or would I switch up to be more palatable to this new audience? Would I *show* them what I believed by being me, and let belonging figure itself out? Or would I *tell* them what I believed to make people feel more comfortable? Would I choose to live in authenticity? Or would I put on a performance?

For better or worse, I chose to be true to me.

———————

WHEN BELIEF BECOMES THE boundary, we had better be careful about how we authenticate that belief. I am not arguing about matters of *salvation* here. I am speaking of *belonging*. If belonging is merely a matter of saying the right things with the right credentials, it's easy to target a group for your own personal gain.

By this point, it is well known that Republican politicians cannot sustain any level of electoral success without carrying the white evangelical voting bloc. Every four years, we see presidential hopefuls making the normal rounds to try and shore up support for their campaigns. They'll visit convocations and chapels at conservative evangelical universities. Maybe a stop or two at a denominational convention or a pastor's conference somewhere. They speak on religious liberty and family values and then head on their merry way. Whether or not they *believe* the things they say is almost immaterial. People find comfort in politicians being willing to *say* the things.

When this happens, a great deal of folks find themselves in community with people they would have loudly condemned a short time ago. Because now? Those people are *saying the right things*.

This reeks of a lack of integrity. It looks funny in the light. It's hard to take a community like that seriously. So fewer and fewer people do each day.

———————

I HAVE THIS RUNNING joke about my desire to become the next great token Black conservative grifter.

It's one of those things I do because I find a bit of amusement in the way society churns through these figures. Some Black people who are willing to take loud and proud stands for conservative "family values" and speak "hard truths" to (read: throw stones at) impoverished Black people are platformed by the larger conservative movement to prove how "not-racist" these talking points and platforms are.

If you enjoy travel, exposure, speaking opportunities, book deals, and the like, I'd imagine it's a pretty sweet gig. And as someone who speaks a fair amount and has authored the book you are currently reading? I feel like I fit the criteria.

I am unambiguously Black. It is not something I shy away from. I regularly reflect on and name the ways this impacts how I process the world and am received by those around me. I was raised by Black parents, and I worshiped in Black churches. I participated in extracurricular activities with Black people. I was even educated in Black schools. Until I wasn't anymore.

In middle school, I started attending a predominantly white private school. I ended up attending a predominantly white institution (PWI) for college. The first seminary I attended was a conservative evangelical PWI. Eventually, I graduated from a mainline historically Black college/university (HBCU) and seminary. I'm one of the *many* Black people who have spent more time than they can quantify navigating two worlds. And honestly? I'm pretty good at it. You could say I've been successful in stewarding the opportunities that have come my way.

And in a world where "diversity" is currency, I am sitting on a gold mine.

It wouldn't be too difficult for me to ramp up the anti-Black rhetoric, talk about "the free market," celebrate some imaginary past where people weren't so sensitive and we weren't as "divided," and find myself with a nationally-syndicated column. I can see it. It sounds tempting. But that's not actually what I believe.

I would have to put on a performance to live that sort of lie.

THERE IS AN INTRINSICALLY performative aspect of religion. That's not an inherently bad thing, so long as everyone is in on the agreement.

For instance, in Christianity, we all understand that baptism is a *ritual*. We know that sins aren't really being cleansed by that water. If we are in communities that practice immersion, we know that people are not actually dying and resurrecting before our very eyes. We have agreed that these actions and symbols represent an eternal truth that we wish to participate in.

But what would happen if some people put on performances we never agreed to suspend our disbelief for? This is the predicament that has faced many people of faith throughout the ages.

Belief is a tricky thing to verify. We can write creeds. We can catechize and confirm people. But ultimately, we either have to trust that people are being genuine with us when they tell us certain things, or we have to give them time to show us who they really are. We struggle with that second option for a few reasons.

First of all, we are an impatient people. Time is a finite resource, and none of us knows exactly how much of it we have left. If the choices before us are either to observe someone for some unspecified amount of time to learn about who they are or to simply trust their word? Most of us would rather be able to take someone's word for it, even if we recognize the risk at hand.

Secondly, when the goal is to accumulate converts, we'll often incentivize shortcuts. It's sort of like having a chore list where completion is the prerequisite to some sort of reward, like going outside or getting an allowance. Sometimes, those dishes won't get washed thoroughly. Some of those clothes are getting kicked under that bed. The appearance of cleanliness might have to suffice if checking these boxes off is all that stands between me and my goals.

Thirdly? Sometimes, we want to give people the benefit of the doubt. We know we're not perfect, and we want to give other people space to be imperfect too. We recognize the power of grace, and so we try to be gracious to other people. It's actually a good quality to have.

But someone with an agenda and no ethics might not have a problem taking advantage of your good qualities.

A COMMUNITY IS ONLY as good as its integrity.

Without some level of agreement on what constitutes belonging, we tend to live in a perpetual state of confusion. We understand this in a fundamental way, and—whether we realize it or not—we typically carry some ideas about how to define our own communities and the ones around us. We usually identify racial communities by phenotypical features. We identify ethnic communities by shared languages, family structures, and the like. We identify religious communities by certain beliefs, rituals, and worship practices. Every day, we walk around building and employing a mental rubric for structuring the world around us into communities.

When we are not in agreement about who we are in community with, other people will decide *for* us. And when we are not clear about what our community requires of us, we will find ourselves bound to people we cannot agree with. This is the state in which many people of faith exist.

It does not have to be this way.

There is no salvation without safety. There is no safety without trust. We are allowed to take a moment when someone's actions and character fail to support their own words.

We do not owe anyone the benefit of the doubt just because they know the right incantations. Character and conduct are fair prerequisites for community. When they are not, we are inviting people who check all the right (or sometimes wrong) boxes to come and put on a performance for us.

Christians have a public relations crisis on our hands. There are a lot of performers in our midst. People who know the right lines have become the stars of the show.

Frederick Douglass, in the *Narrative of the Life of Frederick Douglass*, remarked on the stark differences he observed between the way of Jesus of Nazareth and the Christianity he saw shaping the contours of America when he said, "Between the Christianity of this land and the Christianity of Christ, I recognize the widest possible difference." He went on to lament, "I am filled with unutterable loathing when I contemplate the religious pomp and show, together with the horrible inconsistencies, which everywhere surround me."

We as a people are historically and particularly susceptible to grifters. The boundaries of Christian community are deliberately porous, as our faith has always vacillated between some combination of imperial and adaptable. The result is one in which the *language* has become more recognizable than the *lifestyle*.

The Christian faith gets its name from an epithet. The three times that the word we translate as "Christian" appears in the New Testament, none of them come in a clearly positive context. In Acts 26:28, we see the term "Christian" being used to mock the apostle Paul—even as he is under arrest.

The word "Christian" was not used to describe a powerful people who enjoyed the benefits of hegemony. Instead, it was used to describe a weird group of people who insisted that the actual embodiment of God's power died an excruciating, humiliating death. "Christian" was used to describe people who chose to identify as laughingstocks. But that's not where we find ourselves anymore. The Christianity of this land has differed from that sort of Christianity for quite some time.

I do not care to argue over the rights to the name "Christian." We've had a powerful brand of Christianity around for far too long to relitigate that battle. I do not believe there is *a* Christianity. I believe there are Christian*ities*. At some point, people in this particular field of faith will need to decide which Christianity they'd like to seek belonging in.

There is a Christianity that rewards a suspension of disbelief. Performance is priority. If you know the lines and can learn the blocking, you'll be safe as a cast member for a pretty long while. Grifting is a spiritual gift bestowed upon that assembly. There is belonging to be found among that ensemble.

But there is also a way that speaks of divesting from the centers of power. There is a Christianity that describes a lifestyle of humility. A Christianity that speaks of putting your life on the line so that others can experience wholeness. Walking the walk is the best form of evangelism in this Christianity.

The Christianity of Christ and the Christianity of this land are both Christianities. But they are not the same thing.

The Christianity of this land is an architect of injustice. You can lean on it to sanctify all sorts of bigotry, like second-class citizenship for racial minorities, women, and queer people. Success will depend on your ability to mimic the people who call the shots. It will not require much more of you than learning your lines and saying them on cue. You will not have to alter your beliefs insomuch as you know how to perform when the lights are on.

The Christianity of Christ will demand much more than your performance. It will require that you reevaluate the way you think about the world around you. The way you understand and think of wealth will need to be reexamined. The definition of success will shift for you. People will not recognize you as an adherent of this Christianity until you've shown that everything you value is for sharing with everyone—particularly the most vulnerable.

The Christianity of this land is easy. The Christianity of Christ is not. But, because it's so much bigger than anything we've experienced, it's worth it.

12

Whose Gospel?

Ah yes, that famous second epistle of Jesus to his disciples in Thessalonica!

I THOUGHT I WAS A bad Christian for a second.

The question caught me flat-footed. I was chillin' with a friend. It was a Christian friend though. I suppose he was taking advantage of an opportunity for iron to sharpen iron.

"Where do you find the gospel in the Bible?" he asked.

"I suppose there's four of 'em? Right at the beginning of the New Testament?" I replied, trying to make sure I hadn't missed any councils that may have changed the order or contents of the canon in the last century or so.

"No," came the confident reply, "it's 1 Corinthians 15:3–4."

I opened up the Bible app on my phone. "'For what I received I passed on to you as of first importance: that Christ died for our sins according to the Scriptures, that he was buried, that he was raised on the third day according to the Scriptures . . .'"

"THAT is the gospel!" he said.

I was confused.

I thought the gospel was the part of worship where we shouted. I thought the gospel was the part of the Bible where we got to think about the ways that God made out of no way. The promises we'd seen come to fruition. I thought the gospel was the good news that lifted the weary head. The gospel was always presented to me as a light in the darkness.

Not so. My Christian friend needed me to understand that there was a place for all that, but that the gospel was best understood through the lens of these two verses attributed to the apostle Paul, based on the teaching he received after his period of persecuting the first preachers of the gospel. My friend needed to be sure I knew the *real* gospel.

Up to that point, I'd fallen under the impression that Jesus showed *and* told us what the gospel was *before* Paul ever came into the picture. If we needed an address in the Bible for the gospel, I probably would've looked for one that led me to the words of Jesus. Something like Luke 4:18–19 (New International Version):

> The Spirit of the Lord is on me,
> because he has anointed me
> to proclaim good news to the poor.
> He has sent me to proclaim freedom for the prisoners
> and recovery of sight for the blind,
> to set the oppressed free,
> to proclaim the year of the Lord's favor.

My friend had given me a lot to think about. I didn't want to peddle a false gospel.

THEOLOGY IS FULL OF choices. Some of those choices are conscious, and some of them we make unawares, but we're always choosing *something*. One of those choices is what we're prioritizing in the grand narrative of scripture. Put another way: which lens will shape the faith that so many of us hold so dearly?

The first Christians received their name because of the significance they ascribed to the person of Jesus of Nazareth, a man they claimed was the Son of God. A man who was crucified. A man they insisted rose from the dead and met with *hundreds* of people after having been entombed for days. It is unquestionably true that these claims are central to how the first Christians approached their scripture. And it is reasonable to conclude that these claims are the most important truths of the Christian faith.

But the death of Jesus is not the story of Jesus. The *resurrection* of Jesus is only as significant as the *life* of Jesus. And, if the life of Jesus is of any importance, then we might want to pay attention to what happened during the three decades that preceded his state-sanctioned execution. Those three decades give us the best idea of the sort of life to which he was raised again.

Jesus's death is not good news. And if his resurrection is to be received as gospel, then it must mean his *life* is good news. Jesus's death is a fact. And facts will not feed our faith.

It is the *resurrection* that demands belief. It is the *life* of Jesus that stirs the imagination. The stories that connect us to the life of Jesus serve as the lamps in our own lives. It is these stories that have helped many to discern the presence of God in their realities.

We *know* we will all die as Jesus did. But when you've had your fill of hard times? When you are contemplating the value of pressing on? It is *living* as Jesus did—despite the reality of death—that serves as good news.

The choice before us is whether we will lean on Jesus's life—or his death—as gospel.

———

ELECTION SEASONS ARE ALWAYS funny to me. We spend a lot of time looking at numbers when election season rolls around. Experts spend time, money, and manpower polling thousands of people to see how various demographics are feeling about certain issues and candidates. Economists run a health check on the economy to tell us how our current government is faring. But numbers have a weird way of only telling part of the story.

During my lifetime, as of the publication of this book, there has been exactly *one* election in which the Republican candidate for president of the United States won the most votes. If you read that sentence alone, it might be tough to square that fact with the reality that the Republican candidate for president has still won three of the eight elections that have happened in my life so far.

There is context missing.

There are always more mechanisms, metrics, numbers, and realities to consider when telling a story, so we often have to choose a starting point. If we choose to start from a place of hope and optimism when we look at election seasons, we might assume that one candidate would typically rise to the top of the field and be able to lead with a clear mandate until it is time to select a successor. If you choose to start from a place of cynicism and skepticism, you might conclude there are unsavory factors at play that essentially take the results of these elections out of the hands of the citizens.

The stories we tell are rarely neutral. Most often, they will prioritize someone's outlook while minimizing another's. Whether a story is received as good news or bad news often depends on where you are sitting.

Where you are sitting is a choice for *some*, but the most pressed-for-luck among us? They're not usually choosing their seat.

And that's where the gospel comes into play.

DR. KEVIN YOUNG ONCE tweeted that Jesus's teachings were far closer to socialism than they were to capitalism. A user facetiously replied, *You mean like the verse that says if a man will not work, he shall not eat?*[1]

That reply caught me off guard, because I'd heard that verse, but I couldn't remember Jesus quoting it. So I looked it up just to double-check. Those words were recorded in 2 Thessalonians 3:10, a portion of a letter written by followers of Jesus who learned from followers of Jesus. The author of these words is writing to a new community of faith in a particular city, trying to encourage good conduct among them considering the revelation of Jesus Christ. *At best*, this was a teaching *about* Jesus. It is nearly impossible to understand it as Jesus's teaching without affirming a doctrinal creed that isn't actually found in the Bible.

And so, I replied (also facetiously) with the quote at the top of this chapter: *Ah yes, that famous second epistle of Jesus to his disciples in Thessalonica!*

I realized from the replies to that quip of mine that a lot of us have turned Jesus into a mascot. Many people looked past the joke and rushed to highlight a theological error of mine. *Jesus taught that through the Holy Spirit, who used Paul to write those words!* I thought that was an odd conclusion. Jesus had plenty of opportunities to call people lazy. He spoke with many poor people who might've qualified for government assistance had they occupied that particular social location in our time. He held audiences with people whose only job was studying and teaching. Jesus could've dropped that line in person on a bunch of occasions. But instead, he did stuff like feed giant crowds of people and heal people just because they needed healing.

To insist that Jesus spoke the words in a letter that the Bible attributes to Paul, Silas, and Timothy is a *choice*, and it can only serve to ascribe additional authority to words someone suspects cannot stand on their own.

---

[1] https://twitter.com/darinsmith4golf/status/1615188833422671873

I suspect that many of us make similar choices, whether or not we are aware that we are doing it. We've connected some theological dots to insist that Jesus of Nazareth has said everything that we find in the Bible. It's not hard to connect these dots. Jesus = the Son of God. The Son + the Father = 1. The Son + the Father + the Spirit = 1. The Spirit inspires all scripture. Therefore, the Son = the author of all scripture. (Okay, I lied. It is remarkably difficult to connect those dots, and the Trinity is nearly impossible to explain without doing a heresy unless you quote the Nicene Creed verbatim. And even then, you might still be doing a heresy, depending on which church you ask.)

But none of those dots help feed the hungry. If the theological arguments we use cannot be situated in the lives of the least fortunate among us, they cannot point to good news.

I am not suggesting that we choose to throw away the writings of Paul and the other apostles. I am suggesting, as many before me have, that we choose to read them in light of the life, teachings, and story of Jesus Christ, *and not the other way around.*

If we keep Jesus's life, teachings, and story the main thing in our theology? Then we cannot contain the gospel in two verses of Paul's writing.

We have to stretch our theology to its breaking point. We have to let people ridicule our God-talk. Crucify it. Bury it and move on with our lives. And if our theology is true? If it really points people to God? That won't be the end of it. It will rise again.

JESUS'S DISCIPLES GOT STUFF wrong. Consistently. Judas snitched on Jesus and turned him in to the police. Peter denied he even knew Jesus three times while Jesus was taking charges for the whole crew.

There's a lesson in there. We are going to get things wrong. *Even when we try to share the good news.*

My friend didn't do me any favors that day he told me where to find the gospel in that one spot in Paul's letter. For a while, I almost believed him. I thought that was the only good news I could lean on. And a lot of people still lean on that truncated gospel.

But if we trust Jesus to be a reliable preacher of his own gospel, the story takes on new life.

Jesus's gospel is about the outpouring of the Spirit of God. The same Spirit that hovered over the chaotic waters as God began to shape the world to sustain us is embodied in the person of Jesus. And this is good news *to the poor.* If it is not good news to the most powerless people among us, then the gospel we've chosen is not the gospel of Jesus. If people do not feel freer, more insightful, and loved by the Divine, then we are selling people short. There is more to share.

The gospel is like a game of telephone. There is a message. It is clear and intentionally crafted by the One who began the transmission. But we hear things imperfectly. While many of the key sounds remain the same, a great deal of the clarity has been lost by the time the message reaches a certain point. When we want to know what was actually said, we typically check in with the person who started the message to confirm the integrity of what we received. We laugh at all the many ways things became distorted along the way and wonder how someone thought the original messenger could have possibly said some of the things that were passed on.

That distorted end message? That's where we find ourselves today. Having to figure out how we could've possibly assumed that this is what Jesus meant to pass on to us.

JESUS DID NOT WRITE any letters to any assemblies in the Greek city of Thessalonica. Some of his followers established a community there. Their fingerprints are all over the DNA of that community, and that is not a bad thing. We can learn a lot from that community and how their founders' memories of Jesus helped form their ethics. But we need to understand the reality of humanity. What we receive is not all there is to a message.

The only person who can confirm the integrity of a message is the author.

If I read 1 Corinthians 15:3–4 through the lens of one who was anointed by God with the Spirit of God to proclaim good news to the poor, freedom to the captives and the oppressed, sight for the blind, and favor among the people, then the death of Jesus takes on new meaning.

"Dying for our sins" is an affirmation of the extent to which Jesus was committed to the wholeness of the poor, the blind, the imprisoned, the oppressed, and the disenfranchised. It is for the shortcomings of this world that Jesus died. The many systems that conspire to churn out impoverished, infirm, and excluded people could not accommodate a man as determined to eradicate those disparities as Jesus was. *These* are the sins that put Jesus on the cross. The state did not execute Jesus because some people were adulterers or liars or thieves. The state executed Jesus because he refused to stop standing with the people they'd agreed to forget about.

Jesus's death is not good news. If there is any good news found at the cross, it is that those targeted for intimidation and humiliation by the reality of crucifixion have a friend in Jesus.

Jesus's *life* was good news, and for the downtrodden specifically. And *that* is the miracle of the resurrection. When it looked as though death defeated a champion of the "least of these," the life of that champion refused to submit. The good news is in the reality of life after death.

There is no way that any two verses of scripture can present the fullness of this good news. When Jesus read that excerpt from Isaiah 61 in the synagogue proclaiming the Spirit of God was on him, he was not summarizing the good news. He was announcing it. Jesus uses these words to set the stage for the work that he has been given. The gospel is not merely proclaimed. It is *embodied*.

WHERE YOU FIND THE gospel in the Bible depends on whose gospel you're looking for.

If you are looking for *my* gospel, I can point you to a place or two. If you're looking for my friend's gospel, I'd probably direct you elsewhere.

But, if you're looking for the gospel of Jesus? You're going to need to look *everywhere*.

You'll need to look for the places where people have found themselves pushed to the outskirts of belonging and found a way to nurture beauty anyhow. You'd have to sit with the impoverished who've found new ways of manufacturing sustenance with whatever they've come across. The gospel of Jesus is found where those without sight have been gifted with the ability to sense things we can only hope to imagine. Jesus's good news is with incarcerated people who have not waited on society to call their debt paid in order to find the value in their being. It's found where people who might look like they are down-and-out by society's standards recognize that society's standards are not serving us well.

The gospel of Jesus is found where these people's needs are met and they are allowed to live *safely*. His good news resides in the invitation to see the Spirit of God embodied in people and places that our own cultural expectations invite us to look past on a daily basis.

There is a gospel that centers the reality of death. It will make some sense of who Jesus *was*. And there is a gospel that centers the possibilities of life. It will show you where Jesus *is*.

The gospel of Jesus has been handed down to us through the followers of Jesus. I've chosen to trust them as reliable narrators of that which they have received. This is how community works. However, *what is now* is often greater than *what is received*.

If we want to experience the fullness of the good news that Jesus has in store for all of the creation that was called good, we will need to look at his life. We will need to look at where and how Jesus spent his time. We'll need to examine who and what Jesus affirmed and celebrated. And we'll need to be in a hurry to experience that firsthand in our day and time. Anything short of that is someone else's gospel.

We cannot confuse *what is* with *what has been received*. What has been received is an invitation for us to seek and experience what is. To get from what is received to the path that leads to what is, we'll need to reengage our imaginations.

The faith that shapes tomorrow is on the other side of us choosing to theologize a lil' bit bigger.

Part IV

Faith That Shapes Tomorrow

13

The Future Looks Different

Ain't no capitalism in heaven.

AS I'VE SAID, I'M a bit of a provocateur. But not for nothin'! Typically, if I've designed something to get a reaction out of someone, it's with the intention of getting them to reconsider a previously held assumption.

I like encouraging people to consider new possibilities that exist just beyond the normality they've come to expect.

More often than not, I've considered the reaction I'll get from a particular joke, writing, or thought in advance. It's pretty tough to catch me off guard. I'm usually running my words through a rubric where I evaluate whether I'd say these words in person and whether I'd be willing to get punched in the face over them. This rubric has kept me out of a great deal of trouble.

Sometimes, my calculations are a little bit off. And *boy oh boy*, did I underestimate the sort of response I'd get from this one little tweet I considered a throwaway.

You may remember my previously mentioned, relatively harmless one-liner: *Ain't no capitalism in heaven.*

It was one of those tweets that left my social media orbit a bit quicker than I'd anticipated. It was seen by over a quarter million accounts. A lot of people saw it and passively agreed.

The people who took issue with it though? They did it *loudly*.

People *really* love capitalism.

Some people came to tell me there wouldn't be any socialism in heaven either. Which is cute, I guess. But I didn't say there would be. The tweet didn't mention socialism. Just capitalism.

A few assured me there would in fact be capitalism in heaven. I had someone drop an entire thread in the replies of that tweet making that exact case!

The thing that shocked me the most about the response to this tweet wasn't the fiscally and politically conservative Christians who wanted to make sure everybody knew that socialists belong in hell. It was the many people who claimed to have left Christianity (or at least the institutional church) behind who wanted to point out the errors in these five words. One user pointed out all the instances where wealth was mentioned in the Bible, despite the fact that these instances rarely had anything to do with an eschatological preview of heaven or the "last days." Another pointed to the mention of "streets of gold" in Revelation, despite the fact that the presence of gold does not indicate the presence of capitalism. It sounded like they'd brought the thinking of the churches they'd left behind with them on their way out.

I was saddened by the idea of people leaving the places that had imprisoned their imagination, yet taking the same stunted thinking with them.

———

THE TWEET WAS ABOUT capitalism, but it wasn't *really* about capitalism. It was about taking something so normal to us that we take it as a given (and maybe even God-ordained) and questioning if there is a way to imagine a *good* future without it.

Capitalism is an easy target. To be sure, it has been a major factor in a lot of the things we celebrate in the Western world. But it has also been a major factor in a lot of things that plague us as a society. Perhaps the thing that makes it the easiest target is that it was not developed as an economic philosophy until long after the Bible was collected and canonized. The people who wrote the stories and articulated the thoughts that provided the foundations of our theology *literally* did not have capitalism on their mind. For centuries, people who imagined what an eternal afterlife might look like did so without our current economic framework as a guide. And if they did it before, we can do it again.

Many of the things we take as givens were foreign concepts to the people who authored the texts we now receive as sacred. The concept of ethnicity is quite present in the Bible. But the concept of grouping together ethnicities based on phenotypical observations and assigning them commonalities under the broader categorization of "race" would not be fully developed for over one thousand years after the last book of the Bible was composed. The way we understand marriage and the family is more a product of medieval Western culture than of the landscape of the ancient Near East. The ideas, awareness, and understanding of sexual orientation are also relatively recent developments. The Bible speaks of plenty of sexual acts, but it does not deal with the idea of a person being predisposed to being romantically attracted to people assigned a particular sex. So much of the way that we understand the world is directly attributable to an expanding knowledge bank and therefore our collective imagination.

Our creativity is typically stimulated the most when there are problems to solve.

Exploration shrunk the world in a way. People and cultures were introduced to *wildly different* people and cultures. In order to make sense of these differences, people began to observe and make new categories. Races are human inventions. Around the same time exploration forced people to rethink the way we understood other humans, it presented people with new opportunities to rethink resources and economies.

Capitalism was a choice.

Encountering new lands, cultures, peoples, and resources changed the ways people thought about each of these things. Paradigms shifted. Choices were made. *But this is not the way things always were.* And if it's not the way things always were, then things do not always have to be the way they are now. When our world becomes hostile to creation, it's time to make new choices.

One of the messages of the Bible is that God designed the world to be hospitable for humans. This is why things like natural disasters throughout the Bible are often understood and presented as God's judgment. When we see the planet fail to take care of humans, it is not because humans are an invasive species. It is because humans have adopted a practice that made the world less hospitable for them. This is a problem.

We see this problem come to a head at the crucifixion of Jesus, where the world has become *so* inhospitable because of the practices and systems people have adopted that a righteous man is executed like a criminal.

But resurrection invites us to imagine what new life might look like.

———

IN THE CHRISTIAN TRADITION, the book of Revelation is often where we go to learn about "the last days." People who are ready to get this all over with, the Rapture-ready people, have been reading current events into these symbols for centuries.

It's a *supremely* confusing book, rife with all sorts of symbolism and code words. Interpreters have struggled with it a great deal. But honestly? I think there's one message that helps make sense of all the dramatic stuff in that scroll: *the fullness of what God has always had in store for you lies beyond what you see.*

All the destruction and wiping away that we see in the book is not meant to terrify us for the sake of terrifying us. It is there to let us know that what we've built is standing between us and what God built for us. The message is that, in the last days, God will remove the obstacles we've erected so that we can experience all the things God called good from the very beginning of time.

The apocalypse is the unveiling of all things for what they truly are. The things that have not served us well will be exposed, *even if we enjoy them*. All that remains after this unveiling is paradise. Eden resurrected.

In the Bible, heaven is not merely a continuation of all the things that we enjoy here on earth. It is separation from all the things that have helped to create a hell on earth. This point is illustrated in a short story that Jesus tells in Luke's Gospel.

In the story, a man named Lazarus experiences extreme poverty just outside the gates of a wealthy man's estate. They both die. Lazarus is taken up to paradise with Abraham. The rich man experiences torment from the grave. He asks for Abraham to allow Lazarus, the man who lived destitute just outside of his estate, to sprinkle some water on his tongue. Abraham tells the rich man this isn't possible because there is a chasm fixed between them. He reminds the rich man that, in his lifetime, he had every opportunity to show Lazarus the mercy and kindness he now desperately craves. Ironically, the chasm was the only thing the rich man was allowed to take into eternity. He just found himself experiencing the life of torment on the other side of it.

This short story is an example of the sort of unveiling we see fleshed out in the book of Revelation. It is an invitation to reexamine the choices we are making now in view of the future we hope to experience in the presence of God and all of God's witnesses.

Before capitalism was ever thought of or clearly articulated, excessive wealth in the presence of extreme poverty was presented as the antithesis of paradise. If the Bible is inviting us to imagine an eternity in heaven, it is calling us to envision a *radically* different future.

———

I GOT A TATTOO of a tweet once.

I'll obviously never forget it. Daniel Im tweeted, *If Jesus had a political slogan, what would it be?*[1] Pastor Rich Johnson, a pastor in Ohio, replied to the tweet with the words *on earth as it is in heaven.*[2] I was in the tattoo chair within twenty-four hours. On my left forearm there is a small sketch of the earth with those words written out next to it. *On earth as it is in heaven.*

I knew the Lord's Prayer, but I'd never thought of this one line as the call to action that it was.

In Luke's telling, Jesus gives this prayer after one of his disciples asks how they ought to be praying. Matthew includes the prayer as part of Jesus's Sermon on the Mount. They might not agree on the setting, but they both seem to think this prayer was important enough to share for posterity's sake. It's Matthew's version my tattoo draws from.

After Jesus tells his followers that prayer begins with praising the reputation of God, he tells them that prayer is anchored in the hope of God's reign. The prayer Jesus shares with his followers is that God's jurisdiction might extend over all the earth, just as it does in heaven.

When those who followed Jesus asked how they should spend their time with God, he told them to ask God to remake the world to look more like heaven. Before we get to the concepts of sustenance or forgiveness, the prayer is focused on renewal under God's reign. God's reign is what *brings* the sustenance. Forbearance for the things we've done in the here and now is one of the markers of the new era.

Jesus tells his followers to pray for a fresh start.

---

[1] https://x.com/danielsangi/status/1438528387660713993
[2] https://x.com/richardwestley/status/1438567786905686021

A central tenet of Jesus's message is being reborn. Seeing things with fresh eyes. Having priorities and habits reoriented. Resetting your character. A fundamental change in the way we understand and experience the world is the path to which Jesus invites his followers.

So I got that line tattooed on my forearm. *On earth as it is in heaven.*

I did it as a reminder that my job isn't to get people to focus on living right in hopes of making it to heaven one day. My mission is to invite people to partner with God in remaking the world *right here* to look like the eternity we hope to enjoy after we die.

If the eternity we hope to enjoy is merely an extension of the life we see some people living right now, then Jesus died for nothing. We have nothing to pray about. Jesus wasted his time challenging the rich, young ruler's devotion by suggesting that divesting himself of his earthly wealth was the way to heavenly wealth and becoming his disciple.

Heaven doesn't look like everyone having an abundance of wealth, money, or possessions. Those ideals have been formed by the reality of scarcity, whether manufactured or real.

Heaven isn't endless wealth; *it's the end of scarcity.*

It is a state in which everyone has what they need to survive. Where everyone has their daily bread. If everyone is surviving, then we are *all* thriving. In the reign of God, wholeness is not a zero-sum game. There is room for everyone at the table.

But Jesus's followers aren't just instructed to imagine this paradise for their afterlife. They are instructed to pray for their current situation to reflect that eternal reality. They are invited to help change the world *right now.*

I'M AFRAID OF DYING young. It's a fear I come by honestly. My father died at the age of fifty-two. I was fourteen years old. He experienced a few serious illnesses in his latter years. The prospect of some of those conditions being hereditary has haunted me for the majority of my life so far. It's impacted many of the decisions I've made—even if I didn't realize it at the time. For instance, I became a father *much* younger than he did. In the back of my mind, I figured that if I did go out as early as he did, my kids would have gotten to spend more time with their father.

My father's illnesses showed me a lot about our society. We weren't always ready to accommodate someone experiencing those conditions. I've spent a lot of time operating with that knowledge.

But what if we could build a world that *was* equipped to care for someone like that? What if people didn't have to rely on charity to bury their loved ones because they'd already burned through everything they had (and then some) trying to keep them alive? What if our commitment to community was so strong that we didn't need to concern ourselves with matters like how we'd pay for things? What if the priority was taking care of one another?

My faith isn't just about getting into heaven. My faith is the fuel that drives me to build that kind of world here and now. My faith tells me that the things I imagine are within reach in this lifetime. Because of my faith, I am committed to making sure that my children will not inherit things as they are whenever I do die. They will get to experience things on earth as they are in heaven.

Every single construct is under review. The only rule is that things *have* to look different. They *have* to be better. I cannot continue to passively accept things the way they are. The prayers I've been directed to pray will not allow it.

It is right and natural that my examination starts with the things I've experienced and the things that impact me. But if that is where my examination ends, then I'll merely end up striving to build something that someone else must later tear down to accommodate their own experience.

In the reign of God, *all* of our experiences are taken into consideration. We *all* get a seat at the table. There are no margins to occupy, because genuine love—the commitment to wholeness—is large enough to accommodate everyone. If this is the ethic that binds us, the future has to look different. We will not be able to settle for sociological constructs and philosophies that aim to make sense of the world we've inherited. We won't have to accept scarcity as a given. We will not have to normalize anyone's experience at the expense of another. Our stories will all be valued as causes for celebration and lament. Instead of pathologizing those we struggle to understand, we will trust people to narrate their own experiences for the good of the whole. When we learn from each other, it will be as friends and students, and not as disengaged observers.

We can choose to accept the world we've inherited, or we can choose to partner with the Divine *and* one another in bringing about the age that is to come. We can choose to get with the program, or we can choose to get left behind.

———

WHEN I LOOK AT the chance to partner with God in reshaping the world around me, my fears don't loom as large. My fears are rooted in a world that we've inherited. As I grow more confident in the possibilities that await us in a radically different future, I am less concerned that the traps that ensnared those who came before me are sure to catch me too.

Freed from the burdens of the status quo, we can dream of healthier ways of moving through this world. We don't have to wait until we die to experience pieces of heaven if we take Jesus's model prayer seriously.

So, no. There is no capitalism in heaven. There is no racism or sexism or ableism or classism or phobias of any sort in heaven. There are no rubrics by which we classify some of our neighbors as less than. When scarcity is eliminated, there is no need for any of these things.

And when we recognize the prayer that Jesus shares as an invitation, we can be confident that things will be on earth as they are in heaven. The future is different, and we've been given permission to live in it *now*.

Those who came before us took steps to shape the world we have today. They were theologizin' bigger. We can go and do the same. It is possible to partner with the Divine in making all things new. If faith is the substance of things hoped for and the evidence of things unseen, then dreaming of a radically different future is the essence of being faith-filled. And choosing to operate according to that faith is the definition of faithful.

All that stands between us and the future is the faith to step into it.

14

Living in the Matrix

*Can I talk to y'all about the raggediest theology a lot of us accept uncritically?
We tell people that Jesus died to save us from our sins when we don't even
know what sin is. Too many of us think of sin as just the wrong things we've
done and not the wrong way things are.*

WHEN I WAS A kid, we used to have to say "fib." I don't know
exactly when or where this originated. But saying "lie" was a
bad word. If you accused someone of telling a "lie," you'd better be prepared to deal with the consequences. Not of a false accusation, but of the
consequences of using the l-word. Some stuff you just don't do. And
saying the l-word was one of those things. If you didn't wanna get a stern
look or even a slap, you'd better remember that people didn't tell lies.
They told fibs.

Even if I couldn't follow the logic behind this convention, it didn't
take long for me to understand that it was a nonnegotiable. I could still
violate it, but I understood that I was on the wrong side of right when I
did it.

It's powerful, isn't it? The ways our moral compasses are shaped
without us having a ton of input in the process?

There's a difference between a lie and a fib. A fib is a lie, but on a
minor scale. It's saying you already cleaned your room so you can spend
a little longer outside, hoping you get a chance to clean the room later
before anyone inspects it and finds out about your deception. It's telling

someone they look nice just because you don't know what else to say and don't want to embarrass them. It's that verbal cue you provide to give the impression that you were paying attention to a conversation you checked out of ages ago.

A lie can be any falsehood. It's the misdirection given to an employer when funds are misallocated. The story given to explain away an unpopular political decision, like waging an unwinnable war.

Lies are the stories we tell to prevent people from experiencing the fullness of truth.

Nobody explained it like this to me when I was younger. I had to do a lot of seeking on my own. I understand now though. Our elders wanted us to be sure that we understood the gravity of our accusations.

They'd lived too much life to think that anyone in our situation could get along without a lil' fibbin' here and there. But outright liars? We couldn't abide those. A liar could get you killed.

—————

HOW WOULD YOU DESCRIBE *the difference between sin & evil?* my friend Tim tweeted.[1] Ten words. Fifty-seven characters (Twitter counts spaces as characters). That's all it took for me to recognize a gaping hole in my theology.

I'd been misunderstanding the gravity of a central accusation.

I understood that Christians believe that Jesus came to save them from sin. But I misunderstood what *sin* was in a fundamental way.

For so long, I thought sin was just referring to all the times I messed up. Sin was about the times I said curse words or *fibbed*. Sin was about the times I experienced pleasure in ways that would've made some of the church folks uneasy. Sin was the churchy word we used for no-nos.

———————

[1] https://twitter.com/TimAAmor/status/1618614831963344900

And because I hadn't thought about whether there was any difference between sin and evil, I used them interchangeably. I'd unknowingly been ascribing the word *evil* to myself on and off for *decades*.

It was a gross misunderstanding of my own humanity. Because I hadn't put any real thought to what sin is, I never got the chance to appreciate the fullness of what Jesus came to save us from.

When Tim asked that question, I went to the scriptures like a good church boy is supposed to. I started where the book starts.

I started in the beginning.

HAVE YOU EVER NOTICED why Eve ate that fruit in the garden? Yes, we know there was a crafty talking serpent, but I think it's a bit deeper than that. Eve wasn't an idiot. The story gives a pretty decent amount of insight into her thought process. And honestly? Her thought process made sense.

Eve ate that fruit because it looked good, was edible, *and would give her wisdom*. It's right there in Genesis 3:6. And wisdom is a *good* thing. There are entire books in the Bible dedicated to wisdom. Eve wanted a good thing. At this point in the story, God has called everything (except for loneliness) *good*. Nowhere in the Bible is her desire referred to as *evil*.

If, as most Christians do, you read this episode in the Garden of Eden as the first "sin" recorded in the Bible, then it is important to note that this episode does not condemn Eve's intent. The rest of the story is spent describing the impact of Eve's actions. It is only sin because community is fractured. The first-ever hierarchy is put in place. There is now enmity between different creations that God had called good before sin entered the picture. Sin is not about the intent. The intent was good. Sin is about the impact. The impact was incredibly bad.

In the Christian tradition, we tend to read the serpent as evil. That makes sense. The serpent had bad intentions. His goal was to misrepresent the character of God. The same God who created a self-sustaining paradise for humanity to enjoy in the fullness of the Divine was recast as a tyrant in a matter of moments by this crafty creature.

The same God who let two grown adults live rent free and roam around butt naked eating whatever they wanted from a garden they didn't plant sounds like a stingy control freak when the serpent tells the story.

That mischaracterization is evil. Where harmony, unity, and wholeness exist and a conscious decision is made to destroy that, we've witnessed evil. Evil is the intention to present a barrier to wholeness.

All evil is sin. Not all sin is evil.

If we read the story of Adam and Eve as "original sin," then we see that the sin wasn't so much about the infraction as it was believing a lie about God.

God told Adam not to eat the fruit. It might be worth noting that, at the time that prohibition is given, Eve hasn't entered the story yet. We're left to fill in a blank. Maybe God gives Eve a second instruction that isn't recorded in the story. Maybe Adam warns Eve about literally the only rule that exists. In any case, it's clear that Eve got the message loud and clear. Because, by the time she meets the serpent, the instruction has moved beyond "don't eat that" into the realm of "if you even *touch* that, you gon' die."

I like to imagine that Adam "built a fence around the Torah" when he gave this rule to Eve. In Judaism, there's this rabbinic principle in which the rules are so precious that conventions are put in place to protect them. The effect is that it almost seems like certain rules are being intensified. We see Jesus engaging in a similar practice when he says things like, "You've heard it said 'thou shall not murder,' but I'm sayin' don't even hate nobody" or "If you feel that lust creepin' up, gon' head and pluck that eyeball out." The idea is that we nip something in the bud before it has the opportunity to become a problem for us.

God said, "Don't eat it." Eve received, "Don't touch it."

These are not the conventions of an *evil* couple. Eve's disobedience came because someone else's evil intent caused her to pursue the right thing the wrong way. She was right to want wisdom. She was wrong to do the one thing God told her not to do in order to get it.

One creature's evil intent trapped everyone in a world of sin.

When you recognize sin for what it is—the impact of all the things that keep us from experiencing the wholeness we've been called to—the world you find yourself in might begin to make a little more sense.

The Matrix is everywhere. It is all around us. Even now, in this room. You can see it when you look out your window, or when you turn on your television. You can feel it when you go to work. When you go to church. When you pay your taxes. It is the world that has been pulled over your eyes to blind you from the truth.

These are the words that Morpheus speaks to Neo just before offering him the choice between the blue pill (that would allow him to wake up and believe whatever he wanted) and the red pill (that would allow him to see the whole truth). This is an infamous scene from the 1999 sci-fi box office hit *The Matrix* starring Keanu Reeves in the role of Neo and Laurence Fishburne as Morpheus.

Morpheus goes on to tell Neo that the truth is that he, like everyone else, has been born into bondage. That there is a system he can't even perceive holding his mind captive. The choice between the red pill and the blue pill is the choice between waking up to that system or remaining captive to it.

I think about this scene a lot. I imagine Jesus donning a long, black trench coat and some funny sunglasses with no arms on the side to hold them up perfectly balanced on his nose. He knocks on my door, presenting me with a choice. If I open the door and let this mysterious sage in, he opens my eyes to the ways that my mind has been held captive by the gravest of deceptions. If I ignore the knock at the door, I get to continue with my life as previously scheduled. Believing whatever I want to believe.

Opening that door? This is what salvation looks like to me.

Rebirth is only possible when our eyes are opened to the matrix. When we have the choice between going on with business as usual or breaking free of the prison we were born into.

I'll go to my grave believing that the Bible backs all of this up. It just uses different terms. The Bible doesn't call it a matrix. It just calls it sin. Sin is everywhere. It is all around us. *It is the world that has been pulled over your eyes to blind you from the truth.*

The truth is that you were made to experience the fullness of life. You were created whole. Wholeness is your birthright.

Sin is the condition that stands between you and experiencing that truth. The desire to separate you from that truth is evil. And evil desires can only lead to sinful outcomes.

The paradise known as the Garden of Eden had everything Adam and Eve needed to survive. That's how the Creator made it. Everything was perfectly fine until a creature with an evil intention introduced a falsehood about God's character. Belief in that falsehood is the first time we see sin in the Bible.

It was not by God's design that Adam knew toil in the garden and Eve knew labor pains and that discord was introduced to their union. It was their believing a lie told by someone who had a different definition of paradise that introduced the first consequences. Cain was born into these consequences, as was Abel.

We inherit the systems that those before us built.

In Psalm 51, the psalmist declares that they were shaped in iniquity and conceived in sin. Sin is not merely concerned with our missteps, it is the conditions that conceive us and shape us. Sin is the air we breathe.

In the apostle Paul's theological magnum opus (more popularly known as the letter to the Romans), he says that "the wages of sin is death." In this system that we've inherited, death is the only guarantee.

So much of Christian theology is rooted in this inescapable fact. Death comes for us all, and Paul says that sin is the reason why. We were born into a system that kills everything it touches. "All have sinned," says this apostle. We've all fallen short of the glory of God. None of us has been able to experience the wholeness of what God has called us to.

Jesus offers an invitation to see sin for what it is and pursue the wholeness God called us to at the beginning of creation.

FORGIVE ME FOR THE following spoiler, but you've had literal decades to see *The Matrix*. Neo takes the red pill. He chooses to take the pill that shows him the depth of the matrix.

As he's reaching for the pill—just before he grabs it—Morpheus issues a final advisory: "Remember, all I'm offering is the truth. Nothing more."

Neo grabs the pill and downs it with a glass of water.

"Follow me," says Morpheus.

Only after Neo commits to seeing all things as they are—after he accepts the invitation to receive the truth—does Morpheus consider him ready to become a disciple.

"Discipleship" is a big word in a lot of church circles. It's typically the name we give to whatever programs we employ to aid in whatever the process of developing Christians looks like in our context.

But Jesus's disciples were not Christians. They were not being catechized or learning any of the creeds that would be developed in the centuries following their deaths. They did not carry bound Bibles to church on Sunday. Jesus's disciples were Jewish men from various walks of life around the regions of Galilee and Judea. They did not follow Jesus for confirmation. They followed Jesus because they believed he held a wisdom that would help them see and experience the world in new ways. Jesus embodied a truth that helped them see the world for what it was.

If there is any merit to the claim that Jesus came to save us from sin, then the movie *The Matrix* can help us make sense of the matrix we actually live in. Jesus came to rescue a people who were trapped and did not know it. *That* is the good news he offered. *That* is what inspired a ragtag band of misfits to leave everything behind and follow him. It's the message that drew crowds in the wilderness. This is the mission that, according to the Gospels, drew the suspicion of those in the seats of secular and sacred power alike.

The "sinner's prayer" is not sufficient to capture the gravity of what Jesus accomplished. It is not merely all *my* sins that Jesus has forgiven. It is not just *my* misdeeds that Jesus is worried about. Jesus is worried about *our* misdeeds. It is the systems we've inherited and created to survive in a world that dehumanizes us that Jesus came to make new. It's the way of seeing society through a rigid lens that subjects women to men. It's the ability of the wealthy to exploit everyone who isn't wealthy. Jesus is concerned about the apathy that is so often shown toward disabled people. About the queer people who are often relegated to second-class citizenship or worse. Jesus's solidarity is with the people who find themselves at the bottom of the hierarchies we've created.

Jesus isn't just some *personal* savior waiting for us to make a *personal* decision about our *personal* eternity. The work of Jesus and his disciples wasn't just about making individual converts. He fed people. Healed infirmities. He dealt with the acutely real, physical needs that impacted people's everyday lives. That, as much as anything else, is what inspired people to follow him. He's a man on a universal mission, inviting everyone to wake up to the truth: that the Creator of heaven and earth has so much more for us if we would only see things for what they are.

———————

REVELATION IS A LETTER describing what it looks like when the matrix falls. When everything is revealed for what it truly is, we see the monsters waging war over and around us.

I like to imagine John the Elder, sitting on the Isle of Patmos where he was exiled, trying to forget these visions we're given in Revelation. But he fails. He just can't unsee all of these vivid images. Because they weren't just visions. He'd had his own red pill experience. He'd seen what the matrix was trying to hide. And it was harrowing. So he begins to write. He explains these images burned into his mind as best as he can. And it's hard to communicate. Because you can't tell somebody about the matrix. They have to see it for themselves.

That's why Jesus doesn't just preach in synagogues, temple courts, and wildernesses. He invites people to follow him. He lets people see and experience life as he does.

When John sees the world as Jesus does, it changes him. Some of the things seem scary at first glance. John doesn't seem scared though. Maybe it's because he's not watching it unfold like a movie. It seems like John can see the whole storyboard at once.

The letter he writes doesn't end with destruction. It ends with all things being made new. He wants us to recognize that the end goal isn't merely our own, personal sin being conquered through divinely inspired self-control. The end is the entire sin matrix being toppled. Every framework we've put in place to make sense of this world around us goes through the purifying fire of God's judgment. Our value systems are torn away and replaced with the currency of wholeness and holiness. The world that has contaminated each and every one of us comes to its end. The reign of God made manifest in our presence is the end goal.

I think John wanted us to understand the fullness of what salvation is. It's not just a personal decision about our personal eternity. John wants us to know that Jesus invited him to make a personal decision about committing to the renewal of all things. Salvation is about deciding that we will live to see the day that God's will is done on earth as it is in heaven.

Jesus died a real death. His death was the ultimate judgment. A final statement that the way that we've set up things here on earth is inhospitable to the presence of God.

His resurrection was a louder statement. In the resurrection of Jesus, the matrix is overcome. The hostility of the world is no match for God's love.

When we accept the invitation to see and experience the world as God does through Jesus of Nazareth, we can call sin what it is. It is the air we breathe. The obstacles that stand between humanity and wholeness. We may not be evil. But what we've inherited does not serve us well. And following Jesus will show us the way to the renewal of all things.

We can see the end of the matrix.

15

Anything Is a Heresy If You Try Hard Enough

Anything is a heresy if you try hard enough. Christmas is the time of year where I try to think of a non-heretical way to say "to redeem humanity, God became a human," and fail to do so. What a dangerous faith I hold. Merry Christmas, beloved!!!

CERTAIN ASPECTS OF THE Christian faith defy explanation.

The more orthodox your expression of Christianity is, the less wiggle room there is for theologizin' before you find yourself in dangerous territory.

Take the Trinity, for example. It is one of the defining marks of (most of) Christianity. At the center of the religious beliefs of billions of people throughout the world is the claim that there is one God that exists in three persons. But I confess ... that's sort of confusing. The Father is God. The Son is God. The Holy Spirit is God. But the Father is not the Son or the Spirit. And the Son is not the Father or the Spirit. And the Spirit is not the Son or the Father. But they're all God.

I'm a man who deals in images. I love me a good analogy. I've tried to break this one thing down every which way I could think of.

I thought about how one element, H_2O, can exist in three states of matter. It is most commonly thought of as a liquid. We call that water.

If you heat water up enough, it turns into a gas. We call it steam, or water vapor. If you freeze that same element, it turns into a solid we call ice. They all share the same chemical composition, yet they're all distinct. But if you let some people tell it, that analogy falls into the territory of heresy. A heresy called modalism, to be specific, in which the three persons of the Trinity are only aspects of God and not distinct persons.

So I tried to dream up another image. I thought of fire and how the flames, the heat, and the light are all fire. But someone told me that was suggesting that two persons of the Trinity were created by the other, as the flames are what produce the heat and light. That does sound sorta like Arianism, which says that the Son came from the Father but didn't always exist with the Father. I'm not even five hundred words into this chapter about heresies, and I've done two accidental heresies already!

I get why we theologize in such a bland fashion. It's dangerous out here, and a lot of times we'd rather be safe than sorry. If you think long and hard enough about God, you might mess around and think something you're not allowed to think.

I don't have the numbers or data to back this up, but I have this working hypothesis: a part of the reason that fewer people are identifying as members of a religion nowadays is because fewer people are willing to ignore the thoughts they regularly think.

I wonder about the many people who've had a hard time reading the creation account in Genesis as historically accurate and scientifically plausible throughout the ages. How many of those people have felt comfortable expressing the way these stories struck them? To be sure, there are plenty of practicing and professing Christian communities where reading those stories literally is not a requirement or expectation. But what about the communities where there *is* an expectation that every story be read and interpreted in a literal, prescriptive fashion? Are there people who've felt pressured to remain silent in their faith communities because they didn't want to find themselves cast out of it? Are there people who've chosen to leave rather than keep their mouths shut?

I think more people are choosing to find belonging in communities where beliefs aren't the boundaries. Others of us have chosen to stay behind and wrestle with these things that increasingly seem to defy explanation. I can't speak for everyone, but it's not because I desire explanations that I call myself a Christian. We have the sciences for that.

I'm a Christian because the story of Jesus contains truths that have transformed the way I view the world. I am a Christian because these stories do not condemn my imagination. In fact, my imagination is both stimulated and redeemed through these stories.

But this imagination of mine can get me in some trouble.

TAKING THE INCARNATION SERIOUSLY is dangerous. This idea that a human baby made of flesh and blood like the rest of us contained the fullness of God is *wild*. The Creator of heaven and earth, wrapped in cloth and using a feeding trough for a cradle. That's how the Christian faith begins, according to the Gospels of Matthew and Luke. It starts with God choosing a young woman named Mary to bring a baby into the world.

When the world seemed inhospitable, God chose it for a home. Think about the implications of that statement. But don't think about it *too* hard. Theologizin' about the nature of Jesus is risky business. You might find yourself in trouble.

If we accept that God's plan for the salvation of humanity was to put on human form, then we might have to reckon with the idea that our humanity is not something to be cast aside or handled recklessly. We might need to go on a journey of reclaiming the fullness of our emotions and traumas, understanding them not as fleshly distractions, but as

God-given indicators of our own health. Human sexuality (or lack thereof) would need to be reexamined in light of the fact that God put on a human body with all the hormones and stages of development that we go through.

Situating God in the human experience is fertile ground for theologizin'.

A God who not only understands but experiences hunger, thirst, weariness, joy, sadness, physical pain, growth, interpersonal relationships, intimacy, betrayal, offense, occasions for celebration, grief, and the full gamut of the human experience is a great deal different from a God who is content to sit on high while looking down low.

In the incarnation, we are confronted with a bizarre proposition. The God that existed before the beginning of time chose to walk among the people as one of their own. What was once thought of as imperceptible became a tangible reality that people could see with their own eyes. Converse with. Even touch. The incarnation suggests that God is indeed *living*. And, for some of us, all of this is a little difficult to square with a God who exists outside the boundaries of time and space.

So every time we theologizers get to talking about the reality of God in the person of Jesus, we get to soundin' just a lil' heretical.

I think we should do it anyway.

———

JESUS WAS BORN AS a Jewish boy. According to Luke's Gospel, he was even circumcised on the eighth day of his life. He lived his life as a Jewish man, observing the festivals, customs, and conventions of his people. Though the Gospels suggest that some Gentiles came to recognize something remarkable (even supernatural) about him, most of the people who followed Jesus during his earthly ministry were Jewish as well. He was executed as a Jewish man by the Roman state. And there is nothing in the text to suggest that he was any less Jewish when he was resurrected.

The fact that the vast majority of people who claim to follow the teachings of this Jewish man today (myself included) do not identify as Jewish is directly attributable to one reality. *Heresy.* Many of the claims of Christian orthodoxy are simply incompatible with the wide-ranging doctrines of a profoundly diverse Jewish belief system.

The Christian faith we've inherited was bequeathed to us by heretics.

Not just any heretics though. We're talking about people who believed that the Spirit of God called them to operate and minister in brand-new ways. One of my favorite stories in the whole Bible is recorded in the second chapter of the Acts of the Apostles. During a (Jewish) festival called Pentecost, a bunch of Jesus's Jewish followers were assembled in a room in Jerusalem. According to the beginning of Acts, they were all gathered in Jerusalem on account of Jesus's instructions.

While they're gathered, a mighty wind comes, and something that looks like flames appears above the heads of the people in the room. A keen observer might connect this to the first time Moses meets God in the wilderness via a burning bush whose flames did not destroy it.

Jesus's disciples received the Holy Spirit in similar fashion. But it's what happens next that always sticks out. These followers of Jesus, newly filled with the Holy Spirit, do something they hadn't anticipated.

They begin to speak about God in new languages. Languages they hadn't known before. They hadn't taken any immersion courses or used Rosetta Stone or the Duolingo app. The same God who'd walked with them in the days, weeks, months, and years leading up to that moment now took residence in their being. And that God enabled them to share the truth of God in brand-new languages.

Languages are far more than words and syllables. They're cultural markers. You can tell a lot about what a people prioritize by the things their language is best equipped to describe. We don't have widely recognized words in the English language to name fruits or animals that are not prevalent in places where English is the primary language. People who are multilingual can attest to the fact that languages are not mathematically precise enough to have one-to-one equivalents for every word or phrase. Sometimes, translation requires choices. In communicating ideas and thoughts across cultures and languages, we must use the best words available to us to present an idea.

This means that anyone who was around to witness the miracle of the Holy Spirit in that Jerusalem upper room on that day of Pentecost heard the same truths presented in a bunch of powerfully different ways. If you are hearing the same thing in different languages—that you do not know or understand—the only way that you can walk in agreement is by faith. You may never understand someone else's culture or language well enough to know exactly what these people heard as the truth of God. But, by faith, you believe that you've been called to the same truth.

The idea of the Holy Spirit empowering people to share God's truth in new languages is a guiding principle for me. It's why I started a podcast called *The New Living Treyslation,* where I use my own vernacular to present biblical literature. I hold a faith that can overcome the boundaries of culture and language. I believe in a God whose goal is not that we would all look and sound the same in the end, but that we can all find community and commonality in the truth that knows no bounds. When I say that "God speaks my language too," it is not a rejection of the faith we have received. It is an affirmation of the meeting ground of a prehistoric truth and my contemporary setting being a legitimate location for doing the work of God-talk.

The only problem is that a lot of that God-talk sounds a whole lot like heresy if you want us all to use the same language.

THERE IS VALUE TO an agreed-upon orthodoxy. When beliefs become boundaries, it is important to name the things that you do and do not believe to orient a community.

But how do we live like this when we account for a Spirit that carries us beyond the boundaries of belonging into *new* understandings of community?

I spend a lot of time looking at the stories in Acts when I'm trying to sort through what a community bound by the Holy Spirit looks like. One thing that always slows me down is the lack of clear creeds or confessions. That's not to say there are no boundaries of belonging. (A married couple *dies* for dishonesty among this new community by the fifth chapter of Acts.) But the boundaries seem to be marked by behavior, rather than by belief. Perhaps a better way of saying this is that belief is inspected through behavior in these early communities.

Another thing that slows me down is that, despite how committed these communities seemed to be to serving each other, meeting needs, and even including more people who sought entry into these communities, they did not seem popular *at all* outside of their communities.

When the Holy Spirit led them to speak new, foreign languages at Pentecost, it must've sounded like babbling—because people mocked them. Stephen gets himself stoned for theologizin' because of these new events. Peter and John find themselves questioned and arrested. As you read these stories, it doesn't take you long to realize that these communities were not heralded as examples of orthodoxy by their contemporaries.

It seems as though, in following Jesus, these people got to theologizin' *so* hard they messed around and did a few heresies.

When I speak of heresy, I'm not using the word to condemn anyone. It's important to note that the idea of orthodoxy is a political convention in a notably real sense. Most notions of Christian orthodoxy were shaped during councils that were convened by a Roman emperor. The idea that a group of people can come together and settle on which dissenting opinions and beliefs are out of bounds is as much a commentary on power and politicking as it is on theology. The heretics are the ones who lose the floor fights on matters of disagreement.

Bishop Yvette Flunder has been known to say that "the only difference between a heretic and a prophet is time." If theologizin' is the act of presenting the truth of God to a people at a particular point in time, then we must recognize that many of the heroes of today's faith were yesterday's heretics.

WHEN WE DEAL WITH God-talk in our native tongues, we must account for the fact that our native tongues are not static. As the culture around us evolves, so does our language. Our understanding of the things happening around us changes.

In 2022 I started writing a newsletter called *The Son Do Move*. I got its name from a sermon by a formerly enslaved preacher named John Jasper. He first preached "De Sun Do Move" in 1878 from the pulpit of Sixth Mount Zion Baptist Church in Richmond, Virginia. For its key text, the sermon uses Joshua 10:13. In the King James, Version, that verse reads:

> And the sun stood still, and the moon stayed, until the people had avenged themselves upon their enemies. Is not this written in the book of Jasher? So the sun stood still in the midst of heaven, and hasted not to go down about a whole day.

His point was simple: God alone holds the power to make the sun stop and start.

His sermon was preached in defiance of the acceptance of heliocentrism (in which the sun sits stationary at the center of the solar system, with Earth revolving around it) over a geocentric universe (in which Earth is the center of the universe and the sun revolves around it). Jasper's fellow ministers were a bit embarrassed by this sermon. There was no need to cling to old doctrines in consideration of new revelation. But Jasper was unrelenting. As if to say, "I know what the Bible says!"

Over 250 years before that sermon was delivered, Galileo Galilei found himself condemned by the Roman Catholic Inquisition for the heresy of heliocentrism. In the time since then, astronomers have vindicated the seventeenth century scientist. But here sat John Jasper, a formerly enslaved preacher willing to stand on the Bible as the authoritative word of God, insisting that it was the *sun* that revolved around the *Earth*. By the standards and politics of his own time, Galileo was a heretic. We now recognize him as legitimately outstanding in his own field. Some even credit him with being a pioneer of the idea that the Bible is authoritative in matters of faith and morals but not science. Few of us would recognize Galileo as a heretic by our own orthodoxy—political or otherwise.

John Jasper's sermon was not scientifically accurate. The sun is not revolving around the earth. *But he was right.* The sun *do* move! It's moving right now!

In the early twentieth century, some four hundred years after the Galileo affair and just after the lifetime of Jasper, we came to understand more about the sun's position in the Milky Way galaxy. Our entire solar system is in revolution!

I am amazed by the ways that our understanding of the world and universe around us impacts our beliefs. Our orthodoxies shift based on the things we come to understand. Sometimes our heretics are even vindicated in the process. Other times, we find out we were right—but not necessarily in the way we thought we were.

It reminded me a lot about what following Jesus has been like for me. Jesus is not located in one fixed position. The invitation that Jesus gave his disciples was not merely "come to me," but "follow me."

If the stories of Jesus's first followers are to be believed, following Jesus requires leaving a whole lot behind. Yes, we learn that relationships and careers and possessions are left behind. But we also learn that the ways people think of and understand God shift dramatically when they follow Jesus.

Whether Jesus is a moving target or the world around us merely changes the things surrounding an eternally stationary Jesus, it's pretty clear that what you see before you meet Jesus ain't the same view you got once you follow him.

———————

PEOPLE OFTEN ASK ME if there's any advice I would give someone going through the process of reevaluating, "deconstructing," or even "decolonizing" their faith. One refrain I keep coming back to is that you cannot do any of that in any worthwhile way until you get comfortable with being called a heretic. We will not be able to wrestle with this faith unless we run the risk of having our walk altered in the aftermath. The people who stand to benefit from your conformity will never encourage you to interrogate your constraints.

I am not suggesting that there is nothing worthwhile in the faith you and I may have inherited. I am affirming that there is more to God than what you've inherited.

If theology is art, then theologizin' is painting outside the lines.

You can paint a pretty picture by staying inside the lines, but it's still a picture someone else gave you. And sometimes, it's *hard* staying inside the lines with the utensils God gave you. Sometimes, you've been uniquely equipped to make a new picture. The new picture might provide someone with a new perspective they wouldn't have come across if you'd exhausted all your energies on staying inside the lines with tools that did not suit you there.

The picture you paint when you stray outside the lines may one day be the picture around which the new lines are drawn.

Your accidental heresy might be the doorway to someone's liberation.

16

Leaning into Mystery

I do not know that God exists. I believe that God exists. I hope that God exists. And I operate as though God exists. My faith is not powered by certainty. My faith is made known when I lean into mystery.

WE TAKE SPADES PRETTY seriously where I'm from. I've seen some *vicious* Spades games. I'm not talking about the usual smack talk—sticking cards to your forehead when you got the big joker and there's nothing anyone can do about it, slamming cards on the table when you know the last five books belong to you, the usual stuff like that. I'm talking about adults (who may or may not have been filled with a spirit of less than holy status) standing up on dining room tables to protest another player reneging.

Spades can get *active*.

How you perform at that table is gonna say a lot about you. *Especially* if it's at a family function or social gathering around people you consider close. You get ran off that Spades table too bad, and people start looking at you different. Come Thanksgiving, the only thing worse than being known as a bad Spades player is being that person who brings that dish nobody asked you to bring (and everyone has silently agreed not to touch). Just like it's better to bring drinks if you can't cook, it's better to pretend you don't know how to play Spades at all if you're not confident in your ability to bid a hand properly.

Since there's so much at stake, you never want to play Spades with a partner you can't trust. If someone is known to underbid a hand, leaving points on the table and sandbagging you in the process? You don't want those problems. Your cousin Ray is always counting queens as books when it's the only card he has in that suit? Ray gotta play with somebody else. Your wife is always cutting your books? Those vows do not apply at the Spades table. It is time to tear asunder.

An ideal Spades partner is someone you have a mutual understanding with. After playing enough with them, you can pretty much tell what they have in their hand by how they bid and how they play their first couple of cards. As you learn more about how they read their hand and trust in their ability to bid accurately and correctly, you can get a bit more sure-footed in your own bidding. When you know they can read the table correctly, you can throw in a nil bid without worrying about whether or not they'll cover you. And if/when y'all do get set? You know you'll be able to rebound.

If you've found a Spades partner you can trust, there's not a table on the planet you're scared to sit at. That's how assuring that relationship is.

And that's how faith works.

At the end of the day, that relationship is built on trust. If you play the game right, you still don't *know* the cards they have in their hand. You can only see the hand you've been dealt. You can make some pretty informed guesses about what they might have based on how they're moving. But a lot of the confidence you have in that partner is because of how you've seen them move in the past. They've shown themselves trustworthy.

The cards you've been dealt only tell part of the story.

EVERY NOW AND THEN someone will ask me how I know God exists. My answer is simple: I don't.

Don't get me wrong, I do *know* God. Whether we define knowing as awareness through observation and inquiry or as developing a relationship with something, I *know* God.

It's that word "exists" that throws that question out of reach for me. Existence is a tricky thing. It's how we name objective reality. For something to exist, we can typically take people from all sorts of walks of life, put them in front of or around that thing, and have them all agree that *yeah, that thing is there.*

I can't do that with God. Not in any sense that would pass our lowest standards of knowledge and objectivity. That doesn't mean that God doesn't exist. It just means that I can't prove it.

If I'm honest with you, I'm not really interested in proving God's existence. I've never felt called to that particular mission. That pursuit cannot feed my faith. I will never grow stronger in my faith by coming across evidence that proves the "existence" of this Divine Being. That's simply not how the supernatural works.

God is not a human. God isn't even human*oid*. There is no physical resemblance between the God of the universe and the humans made in the image of that God. There are no hands and feet of God. God doesn't have lungs. We do not have video or audio recordings of God. We have artistic depictions of God, but there are even some people of faith who consider that sacrilege. We don't know what this being looks like.

God *is* Spirit. And most of us would readily admit that spirits are not perceptible through the five senses allotted to us. There was even a whole movie about a nine-year-old boy named Cole who was able to communicate with spirits. Know what the movie was called? *The Sixth Sense.* In that movie, the young boy deals with the weight of being able to see clearly what no one else could perceive.

As a society, we recognize that many people believe in spirits even as we concede that they cannot definitively or demonstratively prove spirits.

Christianity (in its most orthodox, Trinitarian form) provides an answer for this. Some of you may have already rushed to grab this answer when I said *God is not a human* just a few paragraphs ago. We believe that God is fully known and revealed in Jesus Christ, who is the Son of God. But even that statement admits that the incarnation was remarkable because it made visible what could only be imagined beforehand. Trinitarian beliefs only underscore the impossibility of perceiving God.

How can we prove the existence of something that we can only explain in language shrouded in mystery?

———————

GOD'S NAME IS A verb. Did you know that?

It's tough for us to catch sometimes for a couple of reasons. For starters, most of us are reading translations. Those translations usually just say *God* or *the Lord* when we're talking about God. But the other reason is the one behind why we use the Lord at all. The Lord is the convention translators have developed to render the Hebrew word *Adonai*, and Adonai in itself is a convention used to render the divine name of God. The Hebrew authors used the tetragrammaton, the four letters we identify as YHWH, as God's proper name. People would say "Adonai" (which means "lord") when reading the tetragrammaton out loud to avoid profaning God's name. All that to say, nobody knows for sure how to pronounce God's name. People have rendered guesses for a while, but whether out of inability to pronounce the Name or out of reverence for it, a lot of people don't actually use God's name.

I can relate to that. Most people don't call me by my name either. *Nobody* I actually know calls me by my first name. I share my first name with my father and his father (and now with my son as well). If you call me by my first name, I'll automatically know we're not friends. I have two middle names. I share my first middle name with my father and his father too.

The only people who've ever called me that name did so when I was much younger and my *extremely* British acting teacher decided it was a fitting name for a thespian, so I was "George" when I was around the stage.

But all my family of origin calls and knows me by my second middle name: Amandla. It's the only name I have to myself. I don't share it with my father or my grandfather or my son. In the Nguni languages (Zulu, Xhosa, and a few others), "Amandla" means power. Typically, a leader would cry out, "Amandla!" (power!), and the crowd would respond, "Awethu!" (to the people!). The year I was born, this was a rallying cry in the resistance to apartheid in South Africa. This was the same year Nelson Mandela, a leader of the African National Congress, was released as a political prisoner.

This is the story behind my name. My name is a noun. It means power. More specifically, it means power to the oppressed people. My parents gave me this name as a symbol of hope. The message was that the trials we face do not define us, and that liberation and liberty for all is within reach. But a lot of y'all are probably trying to figure out how to pronounce Amandla correctly, and I got tired of trying to teach people by the third grade. And since my mother loved being different, she'd tacked a suffix on my name— despite me being the only person named Amandla in the family. I was R. G. A. Ferguson III. So by the time I was eight, I was *Trey*. I go by a nickname that highlights the fact that I'm the third of my name. To this day, people who knew me before I turned nine call me Amandla. To people who met me after that (my wife included), I'm Trey. It can get confusing around family functions when my wife and in-laws are calling me Trey and my family of origin is calling me Amandla, but mostly everyone knows they're talking about the same person. Even if I'm not around in-laws, my sister calls me Amandla, but her kids call me Uncle Trey.

There are only a select few people who call me by the name that was meant to describe me. *Power*. Most people know me by the name that describes my relationship (the third) to others. *Trey*.

And so it is with God. God is almost a nickname of sorts. It's what we call the One because of who the One is to us. The One is our god. But that's not how God is introduced to Moses.

In the third chapter of Exodus, when Moses meets God in that burning bush, God tells Moses to go back to Egypt and speak to Pharaoh about releasing the Hebrews to worship in the wilderness. Moses asks a pretty important question. Worship who? Who am I supposed to tell Pharaoh that these people need to worship? Who am I supposed to tell these people they're going to worship? Gods have names. What is your name? Who are you?

God's reply is, "I AM WHO I AM." Some people render that phrase "I WILL BE WHO I WILL BE." God identifies Godself as the very nature and act of being. God is existence itself. God says that *you can trust me to be. When all else fades away, I will still be.* That's how Moses meets God at the Mountain of God. The One who IS has called you to lead people to freedom.

God's name is a verb.

And Moses couldn't prove that. He just had to believe it. When God told Moses to stick his hand in his cloak and pull it out, Moses did it. When God told Moses to throw his staff on the ground, Moses did it. When Moses's hand turned white and his staff turned into a snake, God got to show their power. But it was only in moving as though this being actually existed that Moses learned anything about the character and power of God.

We can't prove God's existence. We can only believe it. When we take steps of belief—doing the things we sense God prompting us to do—we learn more about the character and power of God. That's how we come to trust in God, even as we can't empirically prove God.

God's name is not a noun. It is not a list of propositions to be proven or disproven. It is a simple statement. I Am Who I Am. I Will

Be Who I Will Be. *That* is who God is. Whether or not you believe this statement will not prove or disprove God's existence.

God doesn't even tell Moses what that "Who" is like. God's actual name invites questioning. The only way Moses could come to *know* God was to *test* God.

We, as limited and finite people who use limited, evolving languages, cannot prove God's existence. Only God can, by shaping the ways we view and experience the world. And, from the beginning, God has never shied away from that challenge.

———

THE EXODUS STORY IS an invitation into the mystery of God. A strange God with a questionable name tells Moses, a man who has been on the run for murder, to go back to the place he ran from and speak to the king about letting his enslaved workforce go free so they can worship the strange God with the questionable name in the wilderness. Moses met the strange God with the questionable name in a bush that was on fire (yet not burning up), but the people that Moses was supposed to liberate in order to worship this God don't know this God yet.

So Moses has to do a couple miracles to convince the elders of the people that this God is even a real thing. It's the signs Moses performs—such as turning his staff into a snake and back again—that convince them to believe Moses about this God. Moses doesn't prove God through sharing propositions. He has to show people that he and God are worth trusting.

After Moses convinces the elders of the Hebrews, he goes to Pharaoh for the big ask: "Can I borrow the Hebrews you use to do all your work so we can go and throw a festival for God?"

Pharaoh gives the only sensible reply: "Who the heck is that?! I don't even know this god. No, I'm not lettin' 'em go, silly."

Pharaoh does not lean into the mystery of God: "Who is that? Don't know. Don't care. They not goin'. And now Imma work 'em harder too."

This puts Moses in a tough spot, because he's leaned into the mystery of God. He asks the questions. He lets God show him signs. God gets to show Moses who God is. But Pharaoh already has the supernatural figured out in his own mind. He has gods. He has sorcerers. He doesn't have room to understand a God wired to move a little differently than what he expects. The Hebrews don't either. Not at first.

The people Moses was sent to liberate are big mad. Here comes this dude who claims to be one of them but was raised in Pharaoh's house before he did a big crime and went on the run. Now he's back out of nowhere, talking about some God none of them knows anything about, and they're getting worked harder than ever. They aren't in a hurry to worship the God who orchestrated these circumstances.

But what Pharaoh missed in declining the invitation to pursue this mysterious God was that this God is not the kind of God who caters to the powerful. This is the God who responds to the cries of the helpless. That is who God was, is, and will be. The God that Moses met in the wilderness says that "Imma be who Imma be" and leads Moses right to the scene of an impossible situation between a powerful king and a powerless people *who don't even know this God.*

When God shows who God will be, it's through a series of miracles, signs, and wonders that afflict the powerful, but not the helpless. God takes on the burden of proof. That's not left up to Moses or Aaron or anyone else. The people accept the invitation to lean into the mystery of this God once God has given them a reason to believe. When God is introduced as the help of the helpless, the helpless grow curious.

There's one verse, Exodus 12:38, that always makes me stop and think. The verse tells us that when the Hebrew people leave Egypt, a group of non-Israelites goes with them. I always wonder if they left because the land had been devastated so badly that they had nothing to lose by leaving, or if they left because they believed in this strange God with a questionable name. Or maybe it was both.

Maybe these people saw God step in to help the helpless and now, having found themselves helpless, decided to join the people God had just liberated in solidarity. I don't expect that I'll ever have a definitive answer on this. And that's what makes it so exciting.

THE SAME PEOPLE WHO saw God make a way out of no way in the middle of the Red Sea had doubts when they got to the other side. Miracle after miracle, sign after sign, not too many of them were fully convinced that this strange God with the questionable name actually existed or was as good as advertised.

But God doesn't identify as *I Am Who I'm Believed To Be*. God is called *I Am Who I Am*.

For forty years in the desert, they doubted. But they kept going. Through it all, God kept providing. Water from a rock. Manna from the sky. Quails without hunting. God's character and being was not dependent on the people trusting in it. The only thing impacted by the people's belief, certainty, or lack thereof was their own prospects.

God was still providing. God was still making ways out of no ways. It was just a matter of whether the people trusted God's character and track record enough to walk in and through the way God prepared for them.

It wouldn't have made any difference if the people knew this God existed if they still didn't believe that God would help them in their plight.

THEOLOGIZIN' BIGGER TAKES US beyond the task of proving the unprovable. It calls us to reexamine exactly what we believe. Where do we put our trust?

Trust is a scary thing. It can always be broken. As exciting as the mystery of God is, it can also be unnerving. But until we can learn to walk where we cannot see, we cannot call what we have *faith*. Faith is, by definition, trusting and hoping in that which you cannot perceive with the senses. If you shy away from the mystery, you will never experience faith.

Had Moses not grown curious about this strange God with the questionable name, he may have missed his opportunity to partner with this God. When Moses leaned into the mystery present in that burning bush, he learned that there was more to life than all he'd seen. And he'd seen a lot. He'd been raised in a royal house. Lived the life of a criminal. Rebuilt a life as a shepherd, husband, and father. But one encounter with a strange God in a burning bush with a verb for a name called him into a new life. Moses learned to trust God, even when other people struggled to do the same.

If Moses could've proven that *I Am* was present with them in a real and tangible way, maybe the story would have gone differently. Instead, we have a story about a man who trusts a God he can't always trace. Time and again, God calls Moses to do outlandish things: Go to Egypt and tell the king to let the enslaved go free to worship. Hold out your arms over this sea so that the people can cross it. Beat water out of this rock so that the people can drink.

And each time, Moses trusts God enough to do it. Because *I Am's* character has remained consistent. *I Am* was stepping in to help the helpless the whole time, leading them toward wholeness.

While trust can always be broken, *I Am* has never broken it.

Theologizin' bigger is not about seeing the cards God is holding. It's about partnering with God long enough to know you've found a trustworthy partner. The path to wholeness is paved by the helper who's fully committed to seeing you thrive.

You can play the game boldly when you're confident your partner will cover you.

17

The Rehumanization Project

Theology requires imagination. I do not find any shame in that. The ability to imagine is part of what makes us human. And salvation is, in part, a rehumanization project.

T HAT'S NOT *FAIR!"*

I recall saying those words a ton as a child. I witnessed my children take up the same cause when they were younger. Fairness was a principle they simply wouldn't go without. I saw them work through how to divvy up the french fries between them so that everything was "fair." They made sure that if anyone had to lie down for nap time, *everyone* had to lie down for nap time.

At times, they'd question why I was allowed to do certain things they weren't, like order off a whole different menu when we went to restaurants. Eventually, they came to learn that certain things were reserved for when you got older. Then they learned that certain things were reserved for certain types of people. Slowly but surely, they gained a fuller understanding of how the world works.

Some people verbalize this lesson, and others do not. Whether or not we hear the words, we get the message at some point.

Life's not fair.

The idea of fairness comes embedded in many children. I'd venture to say that it shields them from the innate tendency most children have to look out for their own self-interest. Fairness for children is to say that the only way we can coexist is if we restrain our self-interest to the same degree so that we can all enjoy everything equally.

We come into this world with a pretty healthy idea of how things could be. And then people train it out of us.

This world can be cruel. Because we don't want the people we care about to be unprepared for that reality, we train them to be ready to navigate this cruelty. Since life isn't fair, even the concept of fairness is discarded as a byproduct of naive youthfulness. By the time we're ready to release our wards into this cruel world we've spent their childhoods trying to prepare them for, they move by a totally different code of ethics than the one they had when we first met them.

A great deal of resources are spent trying to form children into functioning members of our society. Our education system often has the effect of giving students *just* enough information while they're in school so that they can take over the systems their parents are running. We hand down jobs, structures, principles, and worldviews.

These great big bundles of opportunity we fuss over and celebrate when they are in nursery school are molded into our likeness throughout childhood, adolescence, and young adulthood.

And in the process, they're often stripped of the imagination that once allowed them to see the world as *fair*.

───────────

WE'VE TURNED THE CONCEPT of imagination into something of a fool's errand. When we call something imaginary, we are often questioning its value. We do not value the imagination. And so, taking time to imagine often seems like an indulgence. A luxury. Prudent people must live in reality.

But, when we cannot afford to spend any time imagining, our imagination atrophies. When we fail to engage it, it withers away.

Society pays a high price for this. When we lose the capacity to imagine, all we have is all there is. Unable to form new ideas and concepts that are not available to the senses, we are stuck with what we currently have.

But there is power in imagination.

I believe that all of creation is the product of the Divine Imagination. Before it was made, God saw the world and everything that calls it home. What was spoken into existence in Genesis 1 was first seen by the All-Seeing One.

I've heard of skeptics suggesting that theists in general (and Christians in particular) worship an imaginary God. This is not altogether untrue. If imagination is the name we give to the concepts we construe apart from the five senses, then a lot of what we believe about God is imaginary. I don't think that's a bad thing. I think it's *exciting*. Imagination is fun!

I remember the fun I used to be able to have with a cardboard box. One time, my sister and I covered one with construction paper and turned it into a whole truck. We'd push each other around in that box. We slid down the stairs in that box. Thanks to the imaginations we were born with, that box was whatever we wanted it to be. Nobody had to teach us to play with that box.

It's been a long time since we played with boxes though. We have our own children who play with boxes now. They'll grow up and wonder when the last time they played with boxes was. It's a curious cycle.

If this God is imaginary, one of the superpowers we've ascribed to the deity of our wildest dreams is the power of imagination. That's how the Bible starts—with God imagining all over the place and speaking things off of the divine sketch pad and into a perceivable reality. According to the first chapter of Genesis—after all the living things on the planet are created—the cherry on top of God's creation is *humanity*.

The creation story tells us that humanity is so special to God, they *make humanity in their own image*. The concept of humans made in the image of God—the *Imago Dei*—is one that many Christians have proudly brought with them straight out of the Genesis creation account and into the present day. And it's a good concept to bring. But what does it mean?

"Ain't nobody seen God." That's a Treyslation of the first part of John 1:18. If those words are to be believed, then God is *by definition* imaginary. We only come to know the God described in these scriptures by faith. That same verse in John goes on to say that the Son—near to the Father's heart—is the One who makes God known to us. John's Gospel then spends another twenty chapters talking about all the things Jesus did (miracles, signs, wonders, and teachings) to show us what God is like.

Where other people see jars for water, Jesus sees vats of new wine and helps others to experience his vision in fullness. When a village sees a woman with a history they feel she ought to be ashamed of, Jesus sees an evangelist and brings those same villagers to belief through her. What people saw as a mere five loaves of bread and two fish, Jesus saw as an all-you-can-eat buffet. Jesus's miracles are rooted in the power of realized imagination that God shows in creation.

To be made in the image of God is to possess the power of imagination.

Imagination is an essential part of our humanity. It is our imagination that built cities and civilizations. Our imagination brought us countless genres of music. People have imagined timeless creations into reality through the culinary, visual, and dramatic arts. Literature born of our God-given imaginations has endured for millennia, across time, space, language, and culture. Imagination brought us the Flintstones and Super Soakers. It brought us more sports than we care to name. Nothing worthwhile came without someone first imagining it.

If imagination is a power, that means it can be used for good *and* bad. The concepts of scarcity and money were imagined. Race is a product of the imagination that has fundamentally reshaped entire societies. Just as imagination has been used to create things that benefit society, it has also been weaponized to benefit a select few.

But imagination cannot be weaponized against a people without first disarming them.

And so entire systems have been devised to whittle away at the imagination. The capacity to imagine a world that values fairness is one of the first things to go. Its partner, justice, isn't too far behind. Pretty soon, we can't imagine much more than what we've been given. What we've been given often encourages us to value the things we would've once called "unfair," like the upper hand in a situation where unbalanced power has become the norm.

Without our realizing it, the imagination has withered. The part of God that was given to us to set us apart from all creation has been neutered.

We have been dehumanized.

———

I REMEMBER THE FIRST time I visited Miami, before I moved here. I was going to visit the University of Miami, where I'd pretty much already decided to go to school. As I prepared for this visit, I read through the part of the packet with directions from the airport to the school's campus. It warned to allow for extra time because one of the roads leading out of the airport was always under construction.

I did end up going to the University of Miami. I moved onto campus a few days before my eighteenth birthday, and I've lived in Miami-Dade County ever since. They finally finished working on that one road, but in the fifteen years since then? They are *always* working on some road.

My car stays dirty because I'm tired of washing it only to have to drive on some road they're tearing up and watching it get re-dirtified in a couple of hours. It's diabolical how they do me down here.

But when I'm fortunate enough to find a road that isn't being worked on, I'm often stuck on a road that feels like it was specifically designed to knock my steering wheel out of alignment. I'm talkin' potholes that gotta be portals to the underworld.

The roads here are either being repaired or need to be. They're either damaged or they're doing damage.

The roads I travel here in Dade County are a lot like the people we might encounter on a regular basis. These people are surrounded by people and places that contain a multitude of stories, and there exists a temptation to speed right through them to reach our destination. It is frustrating when their condition makes the journey less pleasant, even though most folk, including me, use them over and over again with no consideration for the stress that puts on them, which is part of what put them in that condition. It is equally frustrating when doing the work of maintaining and restoring through relationship and mutual accountability then makes my life a little less convenient. But all this frustration belies a simple truth: my community, as currently designed, needs these streets to function. These streets need my community's careful attention and investment to operate at their fullest capacity.

When we do not take care of these roadways, they cannot function as they were designed to. All the resources that were poured into making these roadways are rendered moot if they can't be used as they were originally designed. When they can't be used as designed, it causes traffic jams, inaccessibility, and all sorts of things that can bring a community to a halt.

This is how a world falls apart. Slowly but surely, we begin to take people for granted. We design entire communities and societies around people performing certain functions with the understanding that they will continue to operate a certain way. We don't recognize that the more they get put to use, the more care they require. But the communities and societies we've built will not allow us to slow down to take good care of them. So people operate as something far less than what they were first created to be. Instead of examining the role we might have played in creating their current condition, we grow frustrated and disappointed in the ways they've failed to serve the needs of those of us who are in such a hurry. We condemn them as a nuisance. Or worse. We dehumanize them.

The world begins to fall apart when we rob each other of our humanity. Our humanity is defined by the image of God, our capacity to imagine. When we snuff out the imagination, we condemn ourselves to hell on earth.

IF JESUS IS THE salvation of the world, then he has come to revive our imagination.

Jesus said as much to Nicodemus. In the third chapter of John's Gospel, he relays a conversation between Jesus and Nicodemus—a Jewish leader who was a member of the sect known as the Pharisees. In their discussion, Jesus emphasized the need of "being born again" in order to see the Kingdom of God. In other words, we need a hard reset if we plan on seeing the reign of God.

Nicodemus struggled with understanding what it meant to be reborn. Truth be told, I think a lot of us do too. But using the image of *birth* to talk about experiencing the Kingdom of God is striking to me for one reason in particular: a newborn is a (mostly) blank slate. One of the most formative periods of a human's lifetime is the first few years after they are born. That's when we learn how to see and understand things—largely according to the perspective of the people charged with raising us. It's when we learn how to walk and refine our motor skills. *And it's when our imaginations are most active.* That's the time in our lives before the world begins to erode our sense of fairness. We haven't lost our capacity to spend hours upon hours playing with a box.

I think Jesus is telling Nicodemus that seeing the reign of God requires us to reengage our imaginations. We must reclaim our ability to see more than we can sense. Regaining the childlike belief that we can make it happen if we can only imagine it is the first step to seeing the Kingdom of God. We have to be able to imagine new ways of experiencing community. Reshaping the systems, habits, relationships, and expectations around us to reflect God's commitment to the wholeness of all creation is the faith that Jesus is inviting Nicodemus and everyone else to participate in.

The salvation that Jesus offers from the world of sin is one in which we factory reset our imaginations and build a new world of existing on earth as it is in heaven. The invitation to faith is to trust in the character and power of a God who sees good things and then makes them happen. That is the God that we see in the creation detailed in scripture. That is the God that we see made known through Jesus in the Gospels. That is the God that lives inside us through the Holy Spirit.

When Jesus says you must be born of water *and Spirit* to enter God's kingdom, he's saying that our ticket to God's reign is the sure-enough Spirit of God. The same Spirit that hovered over the waters in Genesis fills Jesus's followers in Acts. And that's the same Spirit that Jesus describes as the midwife that delivers us into the Kingdom of God in John's gospel.

When we are born, we have the full capacity for imagination. Ask any child under the age of seven what they want to be when they grow up, and you're likely to hear a range of answers from the same kid. Ask that same child in ten years, and they've likely narrowed the field down to a job or two. Not because they know what they want to do, but because they often feel compelled to narrow it down, and soon. We learn that the time for imagination is winding down and that "real life" is speeding in our direction. In getting ready for "real life," we discard the image/imagination of God that defines our humanity. We lose our humanity to perform a function we may not have been called to perform in the first place.

When we are born *again*, we can see things in brand-new ways, and we can question if what we see is actually fair. We're free to question if the idea of success we've been taught to strive for is really serving us well. We can imagine better ways of showing up for our neighbors. We can imagine again. We are rehumanized.

If the world around us strips us of our imagination, conforming us into cogs in a machine that chews people up and spits them out like interchangeable parts, then God is calling us to remember the image we were first created in. The Divine Imagination calls out to us from the fullness of eternity, drawing us into the possibilities that await us when we remember who we are.

We were made to imagine things so that we can call them into being and call them good. Our imagination can lead us back to the garden designed to sustain us without toil, back before our imagination was captured by one who trained our focus on the quest for dominance. Jesus invites us to be reborn into a world where scarcity is not a reality, but a figment of the imagination we do not wish to realize.

The salvation we have been called to will stir the imagination. It will allow us to see things made new before they are actualized. Like John the Revelator, we can see behind the veil of what *seems to be* and set our minds on what *will be*.

This is the beginning of our rehumanization process.

When we are reborn, we can experience the fullness of God without the obstacles. The limits we've learned are cast aside when we are born of water and Spirit.

Salvation is an act of reclamation and restoration. When Jesus saves us, he helps us reclaim the bits of humanity we've lost. Jesus gives us the ability to imagine good things and the power to realize them here and now. Community without exploitation. A sense of wealth that doesn't demand scarcity. A love that doesn't bleed us dry, but makes us whole. If only we imagine them, we can experience all these things. That's what we were made to do. That's what it means to be human.

If Jesus has the power to save, then we have the power to imagine again. We have the ability to theologize bigger. That is the image of God in us.

Conclusion

THERE IS NO CONCLUSION to theologizin' bigger. It's the never-ending commitment to living and loving more freely each and every day.

Theologizin' bigger is what allows us to marvel at an ancient, sacred text even as we wrestle with it. It celebrates our wrestling as an act of faith, waiting for the moment we're made to walk differently because of the commitment of the One who wrestles with us. In this commitment to theologizin', we recognize that sacred texts are still being written all around us. As we understand the lives that inspired the writings that so many throughout the ages have revered, theologizin' bigger allows us to read our own lives as sacred texts. We can see divine revelation in real time.

Theologizin' bigger is a path to recovering the dignity that the story-telling of human cultures and societies can erode. It's the reclamation of the vantage point God had when they said "let us create" and called that creation good. When we endeavor to see through the lens of the Creator instead of the exclusive lens of culture, we begin to grasp the beauty that exists even (and especially) in our differences.

Theologizin' bigger grants us the courage to maneuver through chaos. In a world where meanings, conventions, and mores are constantly changing, thinking bigger thoughts about God liberates us from false dichotomies and empowers us to reason faithfully in a shifting land-scape. This kind of theologizin' is what allows you to grow with integrity.

It keeps you focused on your commitments even as you remain flexible in your circumstances.

Theologizin' bigger keeps us excited about the future. It calls into question whether things have to stay the way they are. It expands our capacity for redemption and renewal. It helps us to empathize with the many people who struggle under the conditions we've inherited, and it energizes us to work alongside them to eradicate those conditions.

When we theologize bigger, we'll get excited about the times we must reply to tough questions with, "I don't know." We'll understand each of those mysteries as an invitation to keep seeking the fullness we've yet to reach.

Theologizin' bigger is an act of love.

Love is the true essence of God. In fact, one biblical writer goes as far as to assert that God *is* love. If God is love, love must be more stable than a feeling. Love must be eternal. Something we can always count on and strive toward. An essential reality outside of ourselves.

Love is the commitment to wholeness.

If God is love, then that means that God is the commitment to wholeness. Theologizin' bigger is the journey we take to understand God in light of this ultimate commitment. It's how we become better neighbors. It's how we learn to love better.

I'm grateful that you've joined me for this journey. I hope that you'll keep at it. I am committed to your wholeness.

Appendix A

Beyond the Mountain of Known Things[1]

A Reflection on the Quest for Wholeness

I USED TO KNOW A lot.

I was pretty good at knowing things. And so I went in search of more things to know, hoping to satiate an unnamed quest to become the best knower there was. I will not say that I reached that goal. But I did know a lot.

One day, I met someone who did not know much. They did not conduct reconnaissance, as I did, in search of more things to know. They were not on a quest to become the best knower there was. But they *saw* things.

I was jealous. I could not see the things they saw. I leaned on them to tell me of all the things they saw. Beautiful things. Things that fostered hope. Things just beyond the reach of all the many things I knew. Things that seemed impossible, but desirable nonetheless. I wanted to see things too.

I discovered that everything I knew clouded my vision. This caused a great despair. I sat in lament over all of the things I could not see.

---

[1] This essay was first published in *The Son Do Move* newsletter. To receive more writing like this in your inbox while you wait for the next book, you can subscribe to *The Son Do Move* at pastortrey05.com/newsletter.

Nothing I knew helped to fill this growing hole in the depths of my soul. I was no longer interested in knowing. My new mission was to *see*.

And I saw that all of the things that I knew were obstructing my sight. This shook me. Because I saw it. And this seeing brought me a level of joy I had not felt since the first things I knew. It was intoxicating. I endeavored to see more. I could not see through the things I knew. And I could not unknow them. And so I moved. I left the Mountain of Known Things unguarded, because I could not see beyond it. I saw that the world beyond the things I knew was vast. The pace at which the hole in the depths of my soul was growing began to slow as I moved beyond the Mountain of Known Things. I found seeing so much more exhilarating than knowing. And before I knew it, the hole stopped growing. I saw this before I had a chance to know it.

People say that I have changed. That I have untethered myself from the Truth. I have yet to find the words to explain that the Mountain of Known Things is not itself the Truth. The Mountain of Known Things can prohibit you from seeing that the Truth is alive. Indeed, I have changed. Because my desire is now to see, I have seen the Truth. And what I see helps me to follow the Truth where it leads me.

I do not regret my time guarding the Mountain of Known Things, for it was there that I first discovered my need to see. And had I not discovered my need to see, I would not have seen the Truth in all of its glory. I am grateful for whatever ways of being helped usher me to the point of becoming.

The Truth has helped me to recognize the great expanse of all there is beyond the Mountain of Known Things. Because of the Truth, I am free. I have not forgotten the things I knew back by the mountain. I have merely learned to set them aside so that I can see more. See more of the beautiful things. See more of the things that foster hope. Things that seem impossible, but desirable nonetheless. I see many of these things now. And there is so much yet to see.

Appendix B

Hope in a Bigger God[1]

WE MAKE GOD SOUND so small sometimes. Petty. Fragile.

Entire systematic theologies articulating exactly who (or what) God is have been constructed, disseminated, and passed down for centuries now. We got the cute lil' acronyms and everything (looking at you, TULIP). I'll be real with you—that kinda god don't sound too good to me. The love of this god even seems sorta like hate from time to time. This god ain't worried about faith. Certainty is rewarded in his kingdom. Hope is folly in the world ruled by this tiny god. What good is hope when we are already certain about the course this god would take us on?

This god has condemned our imagination. Our imagination has been cast into the lake of fire, where there is weeping and gnashing of teeth. Without imagination, there is no hope. There is just the tomorrow we cannot muster up the energy to look forward to. We dread the future this teeny god has authored for us.

Or maybe it's just me. I could be projecting.

———

IT'S WEIRD. TECHNOLOGY HAS done a number on what we are able to envision for ourselves. The smart phone reshaped the

[1] This essay was first published in *Hope in the 2020s: Encouragement for Our Time* (Grand Rapids, Michigan: Lake Drive Books, 2023).

Western world in the past fifteen years. Twitter gave us access to news headlines faster than ever before. It was dope. At first. But then the news got sort of . . . well . . . depressing. On top of that, social media also gave us access to everyone's thoughts. And if we're being honest? A lot of those thoughts stink. Ain't it funny? The same technology that placed entire libraries into the palms of our hands also made everybody's family reunions super uncomfortable. We gotta decide if we're gonna pretend we didn't see Uncle Jimbo go full Archie Bunker on Facebook or if we're gonna give him a piece of our minds.

The Jetsons had us ready for flying cars by now. The cutting edge of technology left us with people wanting to "make America great again" instead.

Indeed, our imagination is shot.

But what if God is really a creator? And what if humans are really created in the image of God? Not the small, petty, fragile god—but the God whose Spirit hovered over the chaos before the beginning began to begin? What if we can find hope in a bigger God? What if this God is desperately committed to not only saving our souls but also redeeming our imaginations as well? That would require faith in something we have yet to see. That sounds like the type of stuff I'm into.

I GET THE APPEAL of asceticism. Monks are onto something. The fact of the matter is I'm too far down the other road by now. A wife and some kids—I can't just pack up and choose a monastery at this point. So I gotta grind it out here. The idea that we can just leave behind everything we know and live a whole different life though? That's dope. That takes courage. Chasing wholeness over familiarity sounds good until you're faced with the decision yourself. And since many of us cannot choose the monastic life, we must choose another way.

We must choose to live in hope.

The small, petty, fragile god who has arrested, caged, and condemned our imagination is pleased when we stay stuck. His right worship is the status quo. Progress is heresy. Renewal is rejection. Hope is a slippery slope.

If God is a creator, and that Creator made humanity in God's own image, then this other god is a pretender. And so we must abandon that false god. We must tear down his high places and his altars. We must shame his priests.

In *The Fire Next Time*, James Baldwin prophetically declared, "If the concept of God has any validity or any use, it can only be to make us larger, freer, and more loving. If God cannot do this, then it is time we got rid of Him." Because the God of creation never stops creating. Yes, rest is divine. But so is drawing people out of bondage into the wilderness where new identities and conventions are forged among them.

The hope that shapes tomorrow is tied to a bigger God than the one this nation was built under. This gigantic God has been there the whole time, calling for us just beyond the cages the tiny god has constructed around us. This bigger God has freed our imagination from its cell, begging us to come and join them on the other side of our hopelessness. This God offers us hope as liturgy. Progress is not contraband in the reign of this God. Joy and rest are the currencies that matter. They appear whenever true worship—love and justice—has been carried out.

Like a midwife, hope stands ready to deliver us into the waiting arms of a God who is far bigger than we've been able to conceptualize while separated from our imaginations. The God who created—before the beginning began to begin—is present. Holding the hand of our imagination. Ready for a reunion. Ready to inspire. Ready to rehumanize. There is no limit to where hope can lead you, for the God who authored it exists beyond the scope of every thought we've ever had.

There is hope in a bigger God still.

Acknowledgments

THIS BOOK WAS MADE possible by a whole gang of people who never stopped believing the former class clown had something worth saying.

Mom, you are my longest tenured cheerleader. My very first writing role model. I first believed in me because you did. Jamila & Soleil, I just wrote a whole book about imagination, and I still couldn't imagine a better, more supportive pair of sisters if I tried.

Sherry, you never let the "in-law" part stop you from treating me like your son. Thanks for making sure you were the first person with my signature on a book. Tojo, I'm forever appreciative of who you are to me, your daughter, and your grandkids.

Sam & Rob, my parents didn't give me any brothers. But this book doesn't happen if God didn't step in and give me y'all. Ain't no *Theologizin' Bigger* without *Three Black Men*.

Marla Taviano, you probably should've gotten a byline on the cover. You've held my hand through this entire book writing process. I'll never be able to thank you enough.

Alicia Crosby Mack, you helped speak life into my dreams. They're reality now.

Jazz Robertson, you told me I could turn my tweets into a book. You were right.

Benjamin Young, I didn't think joking about a "New Living Treyslation" would help lead to all this, but you did.

A giant thank you to Leta McCollough Seletzky, Rev. Solomon Missouri, and Sharifa Stevens for your feedback on some of the earliest chapters and drafts of this book. Writing in community made this easier.

Zeru Fitsum, I ain't never been as hype as I was when you shared your reaction to the earliest draft of this manuscript. You don't know what that meant to me.

Dr. M. Adryael Tong, you took a glance at this from the corridors of academia and made me feel like I retained a thing or two—but still had my ear to the streets. You a real one.

Holly Bishu, I appreciate you never taking a break in thinking I could get this done.

To the whole Refuge Church family and my mentor & pastor, Dr. Jeremy Upton: thank you for giving me the space and support to be authentically me.

Candice Marie Benbow, once I read *Red Lip Theology*, it didn't make any sense for anyone else to write the foreword for this book. Thank you for blessing me.

To Kate Boyd, Dr. Drew Hart, Camille Hernandez, and Kevin Nye: y'all never shied away from being resources to a first-time author like myself, and I'm forever grateful for you.

Dr. John Allen Newman, you don't know it, but one lecture from you helped set this all in motion.

A special shout-out to my STVU family. Glad I trusted the process.

I took a bit of a gamble in crowdfunding the publishing costs of this book. Thanks to each and every contributor who helped that gamble pay off. I think I'm prouder of the way the community showed up to support this book when it was just an idea than I am of the actual writing in the book.

Dr. David Morris, I appreciate you trusting that a guy like me was worth publishing. This has been a dope experience.

Thank you, reader. You could be doing anything right now. And you chose to read all this. That's incredibly humbling.

Finally, to my dear wife: this book never happens if you didn't insist that I was capable of writing one. You bring out the best in me. Thank you for demanding that I share some of it with the world, even when I felt like doing the opposite. I know that love is the commitment to wholeness in part because of how you love me. It's an honor to love you right back, Jessica.

About the Author

TREY FERGUSON IS A minister, writer, and speaker, with an MDiv from the Samuel DeWitt Proctor School of Theology at Virginia Union University. His thoughts on faith in an evolving world can be found on the *Three Black Men: Theology, Culture, and the World around Us* and *New Living Treyslation* podcasts, in *The Son Do Move* newsletter, and @pastortrey05 on social media. He lives in South Florida with his wife and three children. Learn more at pastortrey05.com.

About Lake Drive Books

L AKE DRIVE BOOKS IS an independent publishing company offering books that help you heal, grow, and discover.

We champion books about values and strategies, not ideologies, and authors who are spiritually rich, contextually intelligent, and focused on human flourishing. We want to help readers feel seen.

If you like this or any of our other books at lakedrivebooks.com, we could use your help: please follow our authors on social media, subscribe to their newsletters, and tell others what you think of their remarkable writing.

Made in the USA
Las Vegas, NV
09 February 2024

85507666R00132